POSITIVE
RISK

POSITIVE
RISK

How Smart Women Use Passion
to Break Through Their Fears

BARBARA STOKER

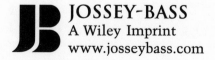

JOSSEY-BASS
A Wiley Imprint
www.josseybass.com

Published by Jossey-Bass
A Wiley Imprint
989 Market Street, San Francisco, CA 94103-1741   www.josseybass.com

Jossey-Bass books and products are available through most bookstores. To contact Jossey-Bass directly call our Customer Care Department within the U.S. at 800-956-7739, outside the U.S. at 317-572-3986, or fax 317-572-4002.

Jossey-Bass also publishes its books in a variety of electronic formats. Some content that appears in print may not be available in electronic books.

Mountain drawing on p. ii is by George O'Malley. Used by permission.

Library of Congress Cataloging-in-Publication Data

Stoker, Barbara.
   Positive risk : how smart women use passion to break through their fears / Barbara Stoker.
      p. cm.
   Includes bibliographical references (p.   ) and index.
   ISBN-13: 978-0-7879-8293-5 (alk. paper)
   ISBN-10: 0-7879-8293-8 (alk. paper)
   1. Women—Psychology. 2. Risk-taking (Psychology) I. Title.
   HQ1206.S858 2006
   305.42—dc22

                                    2005028783

Printed in the United States of America
FIRST EDITION
HB Printing   10 9 8 7 6 5 4 3 2 1

Contents

Thank you from the bottom of my heart to all of the wonderful people who continue to support me. You are the finest climbing team that any individual has had the privilege to work with. It is your ongoing belief in me that has allowed me to accomplish so much:

Brian, my champion

Connor, my philosopher

Joey, my professor

Judith, my coach

Julie, my adviser

Leslie, my mentor

Nick, my negotiator

Shayna, my connection

Suzy, my friend

Valari, my twin spirit

POSITIVE
RISK

1

The Crux Move

The Monster Within

My fingers are jammed into a tiny crack as I press the edge of my climbing shoe against a sliver of rock. This route is at the upper end of my skill range; success here will take me to the next level in my ability. I have been climbing strong today, but now I'm approaching the most important and difficult part of the climb. Navigate this overhang, and I'll make it to the top. Misjudge it, and the best I can hope for is to escape unscathed and call it a day. I'm at the pivotal point of any climb, known as the *crux move.*

I feel my right foot slipping. I shift my weight to rebalance. What was I thinking, picking a route this difficult? It's pointless to ask the mountain to be easier; I must become a better climber. Still, this space between comfort and challenge is hard.

I stop, take some deep breaths, and assess my situation. I'm two hundred feet above the ground with the full weight of my body supported by a quarter-inch of granite. The muscles in my calves are starting to quiver. Elvis is alive, and his moves are in my legs. I'm under an overhang that juts out seemingly into eternity. My heart races when I realize the tremendous amount of faith I've placed in my own abilities.

Time stands still as I try to cut a deal with this rock. Adrenaline races through my body; my lips and mouth are dry. Strategy is as critical as execution. Quickly I determine the next few moves that will get me through the crux. This is a chess game played on a granite board with a stopwatch ticking. I move into position under the roof.

I waver for an instant and for the first time wonder if I'm in over my head. In that moment of self-doubt, I hear a haunting whisper from the monster that hides in the recesses of my mind: *This is beyond you. You're not good enough—if you move, you'll fall.* Now that I've allowed myself to hear the monster taunting me, I can't stop listening. The voice grows louder: *You don't have what it takes. You'd better quit.* I tell myself that this voice of the monster within is only my own self-induced sabotage.

I know from experience that although these next few moves are risky, taking the time to indulge my doubts poses an even greater risk, an invisible risk. I need all the energy I have, and the clock is running. Every second I waste listening to that voice, I burn up precious strength. Hesitating and "holding on" virtually sentences me to a fall. My arms are screaming. I am balanced on a pencil-width of rock. Now I realize I can't see above the rock to find a handhold. How much more difficult can this get? I must make a blind move, or the climb ends here. Somehow I've got to find the courage to leave this very slim margin of safety.

If I move, I may fall. But if I don't move, I will certainly fall. The choice is mine alone. If I wait too long, my lack of strength will make the choice for me. It's true: weakness makes cowards of us all.

I choose to climb. Cautiously I remove my left hand from the crack to put some chalk on it so I can get a better grip when I make my attempt. I get that hold back and chalk up my right. Then I swing that arm as far as I can over the ledge, searching for a crack, a minor indentation, a bump. Nothing. Nowhere.

I will myself to stretch farther, to become longer. Finding another centimeter, I search the rock again. There it is! I've got a hold! I move my legs as far up under the overhang as they can go. I release my left hand and arch it blindly over the rock to find another hold. My feet swing out. I squeeze and pull with all my strength. An abyss of nothingness lies below. There is nothing but air under me now.

Although I've made that move, I'm still not safe. I make a transition in my technique from sheer strength to delicate placement. I slow my breathing to a more controlled level. To keep the monster within at bay, I maintain a calm mind and stay focused. From my tenuous position, I balance and move my left leg up and over the edge, and then I place my toe into a splinter of rock. It's not much, but it's enough to pull myself from gravity's clutches. I reach safety, pausing for a moment to savor the victory: I have overcome the monster within and made the crux move.

Crux Moves in Life

You must let go to be safe.

On every climb, there is a crux move, the single most difficult move on the climb. It's the point of no return. You either make the move or not—very much like the risks you have to take in life to reach your goals. The premise and the irony are the same: you have to let go of where you are at to make your move. You must take risks to be safe.

Consider:

What crux moves have I faced in my life?

Am I facing any crux moves right now?

Do I listen too much to the monster within?

How do I keep my monster at bay?

2

Why?

Why a Book on Positive Risk?

No mountains can be climbed, no hearts won, and no victories found without risk.

Positive risk is a perspective, an attitude, and a life philosophy that creates a shift away from the negative view of risk that so many of us were taught. This book will help change your perceptions regarding risk taking so that you can begin to better understand how valuable and constructive risks really are. Many of us go to great lengths to avoid risk, yet in reality, it is through taking intelligent risks that we grow, learn, and achieve our dreams, goals, and ambitions. By taking well-thought-out chances, we make a difference in our own lives and those of others. By adopting a positive risk perspective, you will begin to see new possibilities in yourself and the world around you.

How Smart Women Use Passion to Break Through Their Fears

This book will also help you understand how smart women leverage their passion to help them accomplish amazing things. Positive risk will help you discover and tap into your own passions so that you can build your courage, allowing you to take those risks that are important to you.

This ability to call on your passion to push through your fears will enable you to set yourself up for success. We will be exploring passion throughout this book, with a special emphasis on it in Chapters Four and Nine.

A Positive Risk Mind-Set

Your mind-set defines
what you think about.

What you think about defines
what you talk about.

What you talk about defines
what you do.

What you do defines your direction.

Your direction defines your character.

Your character defines your future.

Imagine that at the end of a beautiful walk through the woods, your sweater is covered with burrs, which are difficult to remove. What would be your reaction? Would you be irritated over the fact that the burrs were so embedded—or curious as to how those tiny burrs got so attached. Would your frustration grow to the point of throwing out your sweater—or would your curiosity grow into a passionate interest to the point that you'd get out a magnifying glass to investigate those irritating little burrs? Would you end up tossing the sweater—or become a multimillionaire by inventing Velcro?

Positive risk means keeping an open mind, staying curious, and finding the wisdom in every situation. It is discovering ways to tap into your passion so that you start creating your own opportunities.

Positive Risk Cycle

Risk is not an opportunity to be avoided.
Risk is an unavoidable opportunity.

As you attempt new things, you find new talents. As you find new talents, you discover greater success. With greater success, your confidence builds. As you become more confident, you're willing to risk new things. This, in essence, is the positive risk cycle. The reality is that if you choose the right risk and take it in the smartest way possible, it will create a new opportunity even if that risk doesn't turn out as planned.

Stephanie Lake was a first-year student studying economics at the University of Colorado. Since she had always had a passion for movies, she thought about signing up for an acting class at the university. She was nervous even to try acting because she thought she might not be good enough. Nevertheless, her friends talked her into it. It was fun, but after a couple of classes, she decided that although she liked it and was reasonably talented, acting hadn't grabbed her passion the way she had expected it to.

During one class, she met a friend of a friend, Steve, who was attending the Colorado Film School. The school and the classes it offered sounded intriguing, so the next week she visited it with Steve. Stephanie ended up applying to the film school to take one class. It was one of the required classes, Introduction to Directing. It required that she direct and edit her own short film. Although she enjoyed the directing, what she fell in love with was the editing. Having a distinct dislike for computers, she could not imagine herself ever sitting behind a computer all day. However, at the end of a day editing a movie, she felt as if she'd been there only an hour. After that class, she dropped out of the University of Colorado, left economics behind, and started at the Colorado Film School full time.

Stephanie had found her passion. And the reason she found it was that she took one risk after another based on her interest, each leading her down a new path, each bringing her more in alignment with her passion. She has become so talented at editing that several studios in California are talking with her, and she hopes to move to Hollywood with a firm job offer in hand.

What would have happened if Stephanie had never taken the risk of trying that first acting class? Would she have ever found her passion in editing? Would she have become an economist and always regretted that she'd not become an actress? When she moves to Hollywood, will her film editing lead her to another passion? It's hard to say; however, with each new risk we are willing to take based on our passion, we start a new positive risk cycle. That first risk of taking an acting class did not turn out at all the way Stephanie had hoped: it turned out better. As we risk, we learn more about ourselves; we find new likes and dislikes, and we uncover new skills and passions.

We all have hopes, talents, and dreams that require us to risk. Deep inside, we want to make a difference, and not just in our own lives but also in the lives of others. Just as we want to give more, we want more out of life. Positive risk is how you can create the meaningful life you want. Success is hard-won victories achieved by ordinary people who take one risk at a time toward their goal.

Appreciative Inquiry Perspective

> I know for sure that what we
> dwell on is who we become.
> —*Oprah Winfrey*

When I consult with clients on achieving their strategic agendas, I use an appreciative inquiry (AI) model. AI is a positive-based change management process: it is the art of looking at what's working within an organization to identify its core strengths, talents, and passions. This is quite different from the traditional deficit approach, which focuses on what's wrong, why it's wrong, and what we need to do to fix it. The deficit model misses the critical step of focusing on what's the right thing to do.

Most of us have been using this negative approach (what isn't working) for so long that it has become a habit. When people say, "Be realistic," we understand that they mean we should stop being so optimistic and "stop being a Pollyanna looking at life through rose-colored glasses." When people say, "Be realistic," we interpret this as the need to become more negative. What if we began interpreting "be more realistic" as "be more positive"?

Making the shift from a deficit base to a positive base often feels quite radical. But I can assure you that the measurable increases in results for organizations and individuals are dramatic when they shift to a positive model.

Positive risk incorporates several AI components. This book will help you uncover your positive core, which is made up of your own unique strengths, talents, and passions. By understanding your positive core, you will be able to push through those fears that hold you back and help you achieve your goals and dreams.

Why a Book on Positive Risk for Women?

> I would venture to guess that Anon, who wrote so many poems without signing them, was a woman.
> —*Virginia Woolf*

It's not that women don't risk; we do. It's that women tend to underrisk compared to our potential. Even smart, talented, and savvy women who are fully qualified to take a higher level of risk often tend to hold back. This book explores what stops us and how we can effectively take personal and professional risks that will make a difference in our lives.

As women, we often get caught up in the deficit-based model. As positive and supportive as we may be to everyone else, we are often not as kind to ourselves. I've said that I'd never allow anyone to speak to me the way I speak to myself.

We tend to overemphasize the negatives in our lives by focusing on our mistakes and what we don't get done. This inevitably leads to an unnecessarily high level of frustration over not accomplishing more. If you had an extra minute in your day, chances are you'd want to sit down in your favorite chair and enjoy it. However, on your way, you may end up making coffee, baking cookies, changing a light bulb, or anything else. Let's face it: women are fabulous multitaskers, and we get a lot done in twenty-four hours. Most women have a hundred things on their to-do list every day. When we get ninety-five done, do we go to bed early, patting ourselves on the back over how much we've accomplished? No! Most of us go to bed late, focus on the five things we didn't accomplish, think about our mistakes, and dwell on all that we need to get done the next day.

This is so prevalent that I wrote *A Woman with a Minute . . .* This book uses charming color illustrations by Anita Bartlett that create a virtual picture book that walks through the craziness of life for women today. Although this book takes a humorous approach to the multidimensional lives we all lead, it accurately captures the essence of why women tend to underrisk. If every day we continue to not give ourselves the credit we deserve, then there is no way we can feel as confident as we deserve. I've found that the percentage of women who fall into this negative trap is far greater than the percentage of men who do.

There are many reasons for this. A roundup of recent research regarding the gender gap finds that women's stress hormones and blood pressure tend to remain elevated at day's end; in contrast, men's diminish after work. Eighty-five percent of working moms said they felt guilty about combining work and family (compared to 0 percent of working dads). Many of these differences are attributed to women trying to juggle their multiple and demanding roles: spouse, mother, housekeeper, caretaker, employee, and friend.[1]

In addition, in 2002, women still held only 8 percent of the top executive positions in corporate America, including companies where the CEO is female.[2] The fact that women have not made more progress is amazing considering that women control about 80 percent of household spending and, using their own resources, make up 46 percent of investors. Women buy 81 percent of all products and services, buy 75 percent of all over-the-counter medications, and make 82 percent of all grocery purchases. Forty percent of all business travelers are women. Women head 40 percent of all U.S. households with annual incomes over $60,000. Yet the wage gap between male and female managers actually widened between 1995 and 2000.[3]

Women still struggle to find success in a traditional business environment, aptly expressed by the fact that 22 percent of all women with professional degrees, including M.B.A.s, M.D.s and Ph.D.s, are *not* in the labor market.[4] The percentage of women working at least fifty hours a week is now higher in the United States than in any other country in the world.[5] Looking for success outside the traditional corporate environment, women own roughly 66 percent of all home-based businesses.[6]

All of this contributes to the reason that women tend to look at and react to risk differently from men. We want to contribute in an effective and meaningful way without losing ourselves. We know we're bright enough. We know we have the education. We know we have the tools we need. We certainly work hard enough. So what is keeping us from achieving the kind of success we desire?

The reality is that although women are natural leaders, we are often reluctant to take the risks necessary for personal and professional success. I've seen this from many different perspectives during my thirty-five-year career. For the past ten years, I've researched why so many bright, talented women shy away from taking risks that they want to take and are fully capable of implementing successfully.

Although I arrived at no simple answers after doing extensive quantitative and qualitative research, what I have uncovered is a unique phenomenon that takes place within women. We know intellectually that we are talented and skilled, and we want others to value our strengths and success. Yet the irony is that too often, we are the ones who ignore our strengths, play down our successes, focus on our mistakes, devalue our own accomplishments, and refuse to give ourselves the credit we've earned.

One key to positive risk is self-confidence, because no one can predict the course or outcome of a risk. To take a risk means that you must have a significant amount of self-esteem and be willing to trust your own ability and resourcefulness to see the risk through—no matter what.

These tendencies create a phenomenon where women who have the talent, skill, and courage to risk hold back because they can't see their own potential. This book was written to awaken the leader within you. You will learn how to develop your positive voice so that it becomes louder than the whisper that you hear from the monster within.

It's Never Too Late

It's never too late to become the
person you want to be.

Many Chances

Why am I writing this book now? To bust the
myth that it is never too late to take a risk. Nancy
Wells Hamilton is a partner in the litigation section of the Jackson Walker law firm in Houston,
Texas. Her expertise is in complex commercial
cases, intellectual property, and First Amendment
law. Nancy along with her partner, Chip Babcock,
represented Oprah Winfrey during the famous
Texas Cattlemen beef case in Amarillo, Texas, in
1998, which affirmed the right of a person to
feely speak his or her opinion without fear of
prosecution. (Winfrey had said on her show that
the fact that cattlemen fed ground animal parts
to cattle "stopped [her] cold from eating another
burger.") Chip was the lead attorney, and Nancy
held the second chair, sitting next to Oprah, during the six-week trial. The case was won with a
jury verdict in unfriendly cattle country.

Nancy had started law school in the fall of
1980 in Chicago at Chicago-Kent College of Law.

Then she met the man of her dreams, got married, and moved with him to Houston, Texas. She transferred to the University of Houston Law School in 1981 and was scheduled to finish her degree in 1983.

Life, however, had other plans for Nancy: she had a baby in April 1983, interrupting her final semester. She tried going back to school to finish up; however, with no family or friends in Texas for support, she decided to put her family first and take a leave of absence from school.

Things didn't go as planned, and in 1987 she found herself working part-time at an equestrian center for five dollars an hour and separated from her husband. During the divorce proceedings, her husband's lawyers asked her to explain why she had never finished law school in an effort to prove she was intentionally being underemployed and therefore earning less than her potential. Nancy believed that no law school would readmit her after a six-year absence, so she explained that too much time had passed; she would not be allowed to continue. But her husband's lawyers wouldn't take her word for it and asked for verification from the law school.

Nancy went to the school and asked for confirmation that she would not be readmitted. But the dean would not provide a letter unless Nancy formally petitioned for readmission. Frustrated and needing only a simple no to her request, she wrote out in longhand on a legal pad her formal request for readmittance to the law school, explaining how her goals and priorities had changed and then changed back again. When she submitted her petition, the dean informed her that she would be allowed to address the committee that would make the decision. Nancy believed she would be turned down, and seeing no reason to meet with the committee she declined the interview. She simply waited for the letter that would confirm what she already knew.

The letter never came. Instead, the dean called to inform her that the committee had met: on the basis of her petition, she would be readmitted. Stunned and speechless at this turn of events, she wondered how she was going to deal with going back to law school after a six-year absence. Unconvinced that she would be able to manage it all, she asked the school if she could return on a part-time basis. This time she got her no. It seemed the committee was a bit worried over the length of time it was taking her to finish her degree.

Divorce often seems like the end of the world, and yet it also provides a new start with new opportunities. Clearly life was telling Nancy that it wasn't too late and she was supposed to take the risk of returning to law school. Accepting her fate and deciding that there was no real mystery to being an attorney, she told herself, "I can figure this out." She jumped back into school, and in 1989, nine years after she had started, Nancy graduated with a law degree, joined Jackson Walker, and went on to successfully represent many high-profile clients, including one of today's most respected women, Oprah.

Role Models

Need more proof that it's never too late? Grandma Moses began painting in her seventies for her own enjoyment because her arthritis had made it too difficult to continue embroidery and needle-work. Louise Arner Boyd became the first woman to fly over the North Pole at the age of sixty-seven. Lillian Carter, mother of President Jimmy Carter, joined the Peace Corps and served for two years in India at the age of sixty-eight. Clara Barton, founder of the American Red Cross, rode mule wagons and worked as a nurse during the Spanish-American War at the age of seventy-six. At the age of seventy-one, Jenny Wood-Allen ran her first marathon, and at age ninety, she completed the London Marathon in eleven hours and thirty-four minutes.

Another wonderful example is Eleanor of Aquitaine, born in 1122. It was said that at the age of nineteen, in an effort to throw her support behind the Crusades, she appeared in Vézelay, France, dressed like an Amazon. She galloped wildly through the crowds on a white horse, urging them to join the Crusades. Another story is that in her later years, she decided she needed to shed her rough knights of their unruly ways. Eleanor created a mock trial in which the court ladies sat on an elevated platform and judged the knights, who were then required to read poems of homage to the women and display proper courting techniques.

After several marriages, Eleanor of Aquitaine eventually wed the future King Henry II, eleven years her junior. However, by 1173, her frustration over two decades of bearing his children, putting up with his infidelities, and, worst of all, having to share her independence and power with him reached the tipping point. She led her three sons in a rebellion against Henry. Her husband, Henry, along with the rest of the Europe, was surprised with this act of aggression so unexpected from a woman. Then at the age of seventy-eight, Eleanor led an army to crush a rebellion against her son, King John of England. Eleanor clearly was a woman who had passion and used it. The moral of her story is that it's never too late to begin.

Some Key Differences Between Men and Women

> If you have any doubts that we live in a society controlled by men, try reading down the index of contributors to a volume of quotations, looking for women's names.
>
> —*Elaine Gill*

My focus in this book is on you and what it takes to set yourself up for success by helping you uncover your positive core and grow into your potential. Although men and women may have the same goal, our approaches and perspectives are quite different. To be successful it's important to understand some of these key differences.

A year ago, my seventeen-year-old son, Connor, decided that he wanted a job and started picking up employment applications. Most of them asked for his qualifications, and coming up with this list was not a problem for him. He thought he might get an interview, so I asked him if he wanted to practice his interviewing skills. He thought it unnecessary but agreed. When I asked him why I might want to hire him, he answered with a list of his qualities, including that he was responsible, resourceful, hard working, and reliable.

When I asked him why I might *not* want to hire him, he paused—and not just for a second but for a minute or two. Finally he asked what I meant. So I explained that some interviewers might ask him what he thought his weaknesses were. Being completely serious, he said that he didn't think he had any. Then he asked me what I thought. Now it was my turn to hesitate. After some deliberation, I carefully mentioned that he has a very specific way of doing some things. He decided I was right and that his weakness was that he was too perfect. Need I say more?

Most men tend to focus on their strengths, hide their weaknesses, play up their successes, place a high value on their accomplishments, take credit for positive outcomes, and relax at the end of a hard day. Women tend to focus on their weaknesses, downplay their accomplishments, give credit to others for positive outcomes, and continue to work at home after a long, hard day. If we women were to take a tip from men, we could learn much that would benefit us in our careers and lives in general. (See Appendix B for more information on the differences between women and men.)

The reality is that women already have what it takes to be successful risk takers. All we need is to be clear about what we want, focus on our positive core, use our passion to push through our fears, and take intelligent risks.

Consider:

Why did I pick up this book?

How do I keep myself positive?

How can I become more curious about things that don't go the way I expect?

How will I continue to challenge myself and try new things?

What new thing am I ready to try now?

When am I too hard on myself?

How will I become as supportive of myself as I am of my friends?

What are some of my strengths, talents, and abilities?

What are some of my passions?

How can I focus more on my successes?

How can I start giving myself the credit I deserve?

Who is it that I'd like to become?

Is there anything I wish I had tried but feel it's too late?
  If so, what?

3

The Positive Risk Premise

Positive Risk Premise

> Positive risk transforms your once-in-a-lifetime opportunities into once-in-a-lifetime successes.

Most of us don't take enough risks. Why? It's human nature to want to feel comfortable, safe, and in control. Risk, by its very definition, makes us feel uncomfortable, insecure, and out of control. The difficulty in taking a significant risk is that it creates a direct and unavoidable internal conflict, which is exaggerated by another aspect of our human nature: our tendency to doubt ourselves too quickly, even though we know we have more strengths, talents, and skills than we are using.

This combination often starts a domino effect. We question ourselves. Internal alarms go off, warning us that we may not have what it takes. We hesitate, and in our hesitation, we allow fear, anger, and ego to slip in. If we don't regain balance quickly, we can become lost, which reinforces our belief that we don't have what it takes. This undermines our true abilities and causes us to underestimate ourselves. This domino effect most often results in our giving up and quitting.

With a true risk, you will never be sure what will happen next or how it will turn out. There is only one thing you can truly count on: yourself. Risk is the difference between how difficult you perceive the challenge to be and how much you believe in your own abilities.

The Positive Risk Premise:
If you underestimate yourself,
then you are overestimating the risk.

The Edge of Preconceived Limits

When you start a project and begin feeling uncomfortable and insecure, it may not be because you lack the ability. It may be that you are simply nearing the edge of your preconceived limits. If so, your self-doubts are coming too early in the game and may not be valid. Your doubts can create a false sense of danger, causing you to unnecessarily question yourself, lose your courage, and give up.

With positive risk, you begin to understand how to become at ease with being uncomfortable. You will acquire the inspiration and the information required to transform your once-in-a-lifetime opportunities into once-in-a-lifetime successes. Keep in mind that positive risk is a dynamic process rather than a linear process. It is constantly evolving along with the new information and wisdom you are acquiring.

Past Victories

Now think of a risk that turned out successfully—one that you are proud that you took. It doesn't necessarily have to be one that turned out just the way you planned (they rarely do). It could be anything. What the risk was doesn't matter as much as why you're proud that you took it. For example, it could be saying yes to that job or saying no to that job; going back to school or dropping out. Take a moment to think about a risk that you are proud of taking.

Visualizing

Focusing on a risk that you're proud of is an important component of positive risk for women. You visualize yourself as a successful risk taker and focus on your accomplishments. The more you see and believe that you are good at taking risks, the more likely it is that you'll take risk successfully in the future.

Tackling a new challenge always involves some risk. And the larger the challenge is, the more significant is the risk. It is easy to begin to feel confused and overwhelmed. It's hard to know where to start, difficult to find the right path, and easy to doubt yourself. In the past, you may have been too afraid to start, too timid to be effective, or too unsure to see the challenge through. There were probably times when it seemed easier to do nothing rather than risk making a mistake. The result may have been letting an opportunity slip through your fingers, only to regret it later. Positive risk allows you not only to transform opportunities into achievements; it allows you to create your own opportunities.

Positive Risk Components

Positive risk turns the impossible into the improbable, becoming the inevitable.

Positive risk creates an intellectual atmosphere in which you look at your situation from multiple perspectives, understand how you may be filtering information, determine a proactive approach, and finally transform your inspiration and information into dynamic action. There are five critical components or abilities of positive risk:

1. Viewing situations from multiple perspectives—the Medicine Wheel

2. Identifying how you filter information—the Myth of Objectivity

3. Taking a proactive versus reactive approach—Taking Charge

4. Transforming information and inspiration into something meaningful—Dynamic Action

5. Breaking out of our own comfortable ruts— the Risk of Complacency

The Medicine Wheel: Viewing Situations from Multiple Perspectives

Perspective, perspective, perspective. Positive risk means looking at the whole picture from multiple angles. The more points of view you are able to consider, the better decision you'll make. Some challenges are more personal in nature, and others are more professional. However, there are few professional risks that don't affect us personally, just as there are few personal risks that don't touch our lives professionally.

Some American Indian tribes use a medicine wheel to look at their challenges from multiple perspectives. They draw a circle in the dirt and place stones, each representing a different point of view, around the circle's edge. With great ceremony, the medicine man places a single eagle's feather in the center of the circle. The feather represents the issue they are facing, and it is looked at from the angle of each stone. Naturally, the perspective changes along with the line of sight. Looking at the feather from only one perspective at a time will offer totally different views: one a sharp edge, one flat, one lightness, one darkness, and others wrapped in shadow.

This may be a valuable analogy for you to use as you are trying to sort through your options. Shayna used the medicine wheel to help her decide which home to buy. The different perspectives she considered included her existing work, potential work, commuting, exercise, mortgage, remodeling, landscaping, friends, pets, play, shopping, and neighbors. Considering her situation from each angle gave her additional information, which she could then use to make a more informed decision.

Risk depends on your point of view. A great friend of mine who has brainstormed many of these concepts with me for hours on end is Brian O'Malley. As a police officer, Brian carried a skateboard painted to match his patrol car. This was over fifteen years ago, and the kids on his beat thought it was cool. But it wasn't long before word got out to the captain that O'Malley was using a new set of unauthorized wheels. He remembers the afternoon the captain called him in and told him he could no longer ride his skateboard with the kids because it was too dangerous. To this day, he wonders how they could they expect him to be a street cop and a member of the SWAT team and then forbid him to ride his skateboard because it was too risky.

Consider this: for every risk you would not consider, is there someone else out there doing it right now? An avid day trader may be highly successful behind a computer screen yet be terrified to speak in front of a group. A gambler might head to Las Vegas with thousands of dollars but would never consider investing in a high-risk technology stock. A college student might not hesitate to leap out of an airplane to skydive but be afraid to approach a stranger to ask for a date.

People and organizations can be quite odd in the way they look at risk. They worry about plane crashes that kill two hundred people a year, yet don't think twice about car accidents that kill more than forty thousand a year. Some people worry about being killed by flesh-eating bacteria (chances are 1 in 1 million), AIDS contracted from a blood transfusion (1 in 96,000), or lightning strikes (1 in 30,000). Yet one out of ten premature deaths are linked to six common behaviors: smoking cigarettes, overeating, misusing alcohol, failing to control high blood pressure, not exercising, and not wearing seat belts in cars.

The same person who says rock climbing is too dangerous might get behind the wheel after a drink or two. Most people think nothing of driving on a two-lane highway with another vehicle headed toward them in another lane at 60 mph. You may be a good driver, yet what about that other driver? You'll be passing within a few feet of each other. A two-second slip in concentration can result in devastation. What one person considers an unacceptable risk, another will jump into without hesitation. To take intelligent risks, it is important to view your own situation from as many perspectives as possible.

The Myth of Objectivity: Identifying How You Filter Information

We all look at risk differently. Let's explore why. Facts provide objective information. Yet the facts mean little out of context. Context is created out of our subjectivity. Depending on whose context you use, the meaning can vary dramatically.

All of us have gone out in search of information. We often use the information that supports our point of view and dismiss any information that doesn't. Politicians (among many others) have refined the spin into an art form. They have honed this skill to such a point that they don't even have to go out and find the right set of facts; they've become so adept that they can actually use the same facts to argue both sides. For example, the fact is that John Smith has risen in the polls by 14 percentage points. Spin A gives us this headline: "John Smith is still losing by a huge 5 percent margin." Spin B offers a different headline: "At the rate John Smith is gaining in the polls, he will be leading by 10 percentage points by next week." Many of us have become increasingly savvy about not believing all we hear from others. But do we put our own opinions through such scrutiny?

If Facts Mean Little Out of Context, Let the Context Begin You wake up to an unexpected ice storm. Every news channel is repeating warnings not to drive. Most of the main roads have been closed, and there are travel advisories posted for the ones still open. In fact you just heard the announcer say, "If you go out, be careful." Do you go to work? Of course not! You aren't going to risk being in an accident just to get to the office.

Perhaps you settle down into a comfortable chair with a great book since your passion is reading. The weather continues to worsen throughout the day. You start wondering if tonight's book auction, which you've looked forward to for months, will be canceled. You desperately want a rare book that is being auctioned off, and you must be there in person to bid. All of a sudden, the roads start looking better to you. Didn't that announcer just say, "If you go out, be careful"? That must mean the roads are getting clearer. Maybe you could make it. No one else is going to be out driving in this storm, so that would make it even safer. Better yet, if not many people are going out, there may be fewer people at the auction to bid against you.

You have begun to hear the information about the roads a little differently based on your own interests. We all do it. It's human nature. However, if you are willing to recognize that your passion for books may be altering the way you are looking at the storm, then you may reconsider before going out. If you are unaware or if you choose to ignore how your passion and interests are filtering the conditions and go out anyway, then you'll be taking a careless chance versus an intelligent risk.

Subjectively Objective The danger doesn't lie in not being objective. The danger lies in *thinking* that you are being objective when you aren't.

Positive risk doesn't require you try to be completely objective. Just the contrary is true: it asks you to recognize that you, like everyone else, are subjectively objective. You are probably aware of this, yet may try to kid yourself or others by saying, "I'm being totally objective about this." If you ever catch yourself saying or thinking this, beware: you are setting yourself up to take an uninformed risk. To dramatically increase your chances of risking successfully, begin challenging yourself, "I know I'm being subjective. How am I filtering this information?"

Taking Charge: Taking a Proactive versus Reactive Approach

Success requires that you make your own choices as often as possible. I do keynotes, workshops, and training around the country on the topic of positive risk. During my programs, I hear example after example from people who have listened to others and followed the wrong path because they lacked the courage to forge their own trail. I have met accountants who wanted to be artists, artists who wanted to teach, teachers who wanted to be attorneys, and attorneys who wanted to be accountants. Each person is different, yet their stories are similar: they all fell into the trap of following someone else, and they all regret not following their own dream.

Positive risk is a dynamic process that requires you to be proactive and make your own choices. It means that if you don't like the direction things are going, it's your job to set a new one. If you aren't happy not making any interest on your money, you need to pull it out of the mattress and invest it. If you think your life is boring, then recognize you are boring and change. It's your responsibility to make your own life exciting.

Climbing Mount Everest is an excellent example of how valuable it is for a person to adapt to harsh conditions. It's an asset because you find new levels of endurance, stamina, and performance. If you haven't attempted climbing the real Mount Everest, then perhaps you've experienced this level of challenge in your own life.

It is important for you to be aware that there are times when learning to adapt to severe conditions is a serious liability. Adapting to an extremely harsh, negative environment should be treated as a temporary challenge. It should be a situation that you get through, become a better person from the experience, and then move on. It should not be accepted as the norm. Too often we find ourselves adapting to and trapped inside difficult environments in our everyday lives. If you are stuck in an abusive relationship or reporting to a boss who harasses you, then you need to take the risk of getting out. It is a much smaller risk to leave than the risk you'll take if you stay in that situation.

If you are unhappy in your job, do something about it. You may decide to accept your job the way it is and look for ways to enjoy it again. You may decide to try to change your job so that it becomes something you can begin to like. Or you may decide to reject your job and start interviewing for a position with a new company. Any of these choices is good, just don't wait around in a job you dislike and then act surprised when you're offered early retirement at the age of thirty-one. When things aren't working, whether it's personally or professionally, you essentially have three choices: accept, change, or reject.

If your specific situation is not working, it's your responsibility to acknowledge what is happening and make a choice. You may choose to *accept* it because it really isn't that bad. You may decide to *change* it, and fix the problems because you want it to work. Or you may decide to *reject* the situation and leave on your own terms.

Each decision poses different kinds of challenges and risks. Any one of these choices may be the right one for varying reasons. Positive risk means that you don't risk out of default. Instead you make a thoughtful, deliberate, and conscious choice about what course of action will be best.

Dynamic Action: Transforming Information and Inspiration into Something Meaningful

When you contemplate a risky venture, two components you'll want to explore are information and inspiration. You may have been taught over the course of a lifetime that all risks can be measured. Although many pieces of the puzzle can be quantified, no one has yet figured out how to measure all aspects of a risk. If everything could be measured and calculated, then it wouldn't really be a risk because you would know exactly how it would turn out. Acquiring the information you need to make smart choices is critically important. If you are taking the risk of buying a new home and trying to decide between two different types of home loans, what you need the most is accurate information.

However, in most cases, the challenge you are considering will not be clear-cut. Information alone is not adequate. It is important to consider other factors and recognize that the passion you have around taking this risk is equally important. In fact, your passion can often determine the outcome.

Inspiration is what will see you through. For every challenge you find overwhelming, look, and you'll find inspiration from others. I found a visual example of this one day when I took my boys to the skateboard park. Kids at every skill level raced around in all directions at every imaginable speed. Some were on skateboards, others on roller blades, and a few on BMX trick bikes. At first I thought, "This is insane. They're all going to crash." Then as I studied the chaos, it was clear each kid had his own place in the system. There was a rhythm to the madness that the kids seemed to understand. What was the common denominator? Passion.

For every skater who looked like a beginner, there was another who knew even less. For every skater I thought was the best, there was one next to him doing an even more difficult stunt. Each kid out there was, at the same time, both a student and teacher to those around them. One minute I'd see one of the experienced skaters giving advice to a younger skater. The next minute when that "expert" lost a bet with Newton's Law of Gravity, it was the younger skater handing out the advice and encouragement.

It was easy to see which ones already knew about intelligent risk taking. They were the ones with the helmets and pads. It was also interesting to see the culture they created around "getting tough." If any one of those kids had taken a hard fall at home, he would have limped inside to Mom tearfully and get sympathy. In the skateboard park, though, there's a different expectation: if you're seriously hurt, we'll help; otherwise, stop whining.

Every skater out there was missing tricks, taking falls, and getting scraped. It was at times hard to watch. No doubt the paramedics make regular stops there. Yet I overheard the kids saying some interesting things to each other: "Start with some easy stuff, and keep your balance. Everybody falls; just get back up." It's good advice for any endeavor. Despite all their mishaps, one fact remained obvious: those without passion leave; those with passion pick themselves up and try again.

The Risk of Complacency: Breaking Out of Our Own Comfortable Ruts

Did you take more risks when you were younger? We all start out with an inherently adventurous spirit, yet too often that spirit fades over time. Each of us faces the danger of getting too comfortable and becoming complacent with our lives. Each of us, when not pushed, sets comfortable, artificial limits for ourselves.

Chances are that when you were younger, you were more willing to try new things and take more risks. We all understand how important it is that parents try to give children the opportunity to explore new interests so that they can find hidden talents. But do you do this for yourself? Isn't it just as important for you to continue to explore new interests and uncover hidden talents so that you can continue to grow?

We all need a push. One of the fastest-growing industries in the United States is personal training. Personal trainers are great for setting up exercise programs that are both safe and effective. Unfortunately, many of us become reliant on a trainer to push us. We depend on this person to tell us to do one more push-up although we all know we *should* do one more push-up. It's just that without their inspiration and motivation, most of us won't do that one more on our own. Why? Because we like to be comfortable, and that last one is hard to do although we know it's the most valuable one. Only by going beyond our limit do we build.

Positive Risk Concepts

A key concept in positive risk is the ability to look beyond the obvious. Most people look at their risk-to-reward ratio, but that is just scratching the surface. It is important to look beyond it to your own courage ratio, which helps you to determine if you have enough passion to push through your fears, allowing you to rise to the challenge. This concept requires that you explore your passions and fears as well as the invisible risks and invisible rewards that are involved in your specific situation. (Both of these concepts are explored in Chapters Four and Five.)

IntelligentRisking Process

Positive risk is a perspective, an attitude, and a life philosophy. It is a mind-set that allows you the ability to see the possibilities in yourself and your life. It may help to look at it as the "want to."

IntelligentRisking is a process that incorporates the specific strategies, tools, and critical questions that will help you determine which risks to take, when to take them, and how to take them in the smartest way possible. Look at it as the "how to." Success comes from blending the "want to" with the "how to." IntelligentRisking builds from four simple strategies, each made up of fifteen critical questions everyone should ask as they consider taking a risk. Chapters Six through Ten look at these strategies, and Appendix A lists all fifteen critical questions.

Consider:

Do I let a few mistakes shake my confidence?

When I get uncomfortable, do I tend to think I'm going in the wrong direction?

How can I get myself more comfortable being uncomfortable?

How can I help myself look at my situation from a variety of perspectives?

How do I tend to filter information?

Do I understand how I am being "subjectively objective"?

How can I be more proactive?

When do I find myself being reactive?

Do I tend to accept, reject, or change situations that aren't working?

How can I better blend information and inspiration to help me take action?

How do I keep from becoming too complacent?

The Courage Ratio

Finding Courage

> Far better it is to dare mighty things,
> to win glorious triumphs, even though
> checkered by failure, than to take rank
> with those poor spirits who neither enjoy
> much nor suffer much, because they
> live in the gray twilight that knows
> not victory nor defeat.
>
> —*Teddy Roosevelt*

Imagine you are walking along one of the beautiful beaches in Acapulco. In the distance, you can see the cliff divers performing their incredible swan dives from a one-hundred-foot ledge. You're thinking, "Wow, that looks like so much fun . . . for them."

You continue on and are now standing on a rock that's just barely sticking up out of the water. The ocean is perfectly clear and warm. You're an excellent swimmer. There are no sharks, not like yesterday. The sun is high, and you're getting hot.

This is the scenario I present in my Positive Risk Keynote and IntelligentRisking workshops. Then I ask the audience to participate. As you read on, consider how you might react. "Raise your hand if you would be willing to dip your toes into the water to cool off." (At this point everyone's hand is raised.) "Would you be willing to jump into the water from one foot? If so, raise your hand and keep your hand up until you personally wouldn't be willing to jump." "Would you be willing to jump in from five feet up?" "Ten feet?" (Some of the hands are going down.) "Fifty feet?" (Most of the hands are down.) "Would you be willing to jump just once from one hundred feet?" (All but one or two hands are down based on their fear of getting hurt or injured.)

This is a straightforward example of a risk-to-reward ratio. As the audience sees the risk go up in relationship to the reward, their hands go down. What if we changed the equation slightly? "Would you consider jumping *just once* from one hundred feet for $1 million in cash, tax free?" Before

I can finish saying "tax free," most of the hands are in the air. However, others are still saying, "No way." Which group would you be in?

Let's change the equation again: "What if I told you that someone you loved more than anyone else in this world was dying and needed an operation that cost $1 million to save his or her life? Would you be willing to jump?"

Most of the people who had still been unwilling to jump change their minds at this point. Within seconds, the entire audience has shifted from, "No way, I won't jump" to, "Sure I'll jump; just show me where." Did the risk of getting hurt or injured change? No. The risk of injury was exactly the same seconds ago as it is right now. What changed? Your passion.

Exploring Your Courage Ratio

Behind every risk is a fear. Behind every reward is a passion. When your passion is greater than your fear, you find your courage:

$$Passion > Fear = Courage$$

The courage ratio takes the risk-to-reward ratio to the next level by exploring the true motivators that lie beneath our behavior. For every risk you're afraid to take, is there someone else out there doing it? Probably. Why would that risk be acceptable to someone else yet not to you? Ask yourself some questions:

✓ What's my problem with this risk?
✓ What's my fear behind the risk?
✓ Why is this reward so meaningful to me?
✓ What's the passion that this reward taps into for me?

Signature Risks

> One isn't necessarily born with courage, but one is born with potential. Without courage, we cannot practice any other virtue with consistency. We can't be kind, true, merciful, generous, or honest.
>
> —*Maya Angelou*

All of us have signature risks—experiences that have defined us in a unique way. One of mine took place while I worked at Hallmark Cards. My degree was in industrial design from the University of Illinois, and my first job was working in the field out of the Chicago office designing stores for Hallmark

Cards. After a few years, I was promoted to assistant product manager and transferred to the home office in Kansas City. My new job then was to get Hallmark into the gift business. Since Hallmark stores are privately owned and not franchised, the shops could and did buy gift items from vendors other than Hallmark.

The assignment was an obvious mountain, but the route was clear: the existing product managers of the various product lines would develop gifts for the program. Although I was close to the bottom of the Hallmark food chain, I met with all the product managers, who agreed to design gifts for the program. It is important to note that none of the product managers reported to me, the gift program was not part of their goals, and it would require a great deal of extra work for them. What did they do? The same thing you and I would have done in their place: they met their own goals, and the gift program waited.

The first year, I got a couple of votive candles and not much more. The second year was promising similar results, so I went to my boss and asked for help, direction, and guidance. I have not forgotten that day more than twenty years ago when he looked me right in the eye and said, "Barbara, if I need to help you, then I don't need you, do I?"

As I walked out of his office, I was both furious and scared. This was my first close-up look at the risk-to-reward ratio and my own fears and passions. My fear was that I was being set up, with the possibility of being fired. My passion was to prove I could do it (without any help from my boss). I had a choice to make: be a victim, or fight back. I chose to fight, and that was a defining moment in my life.

I decided that as my own risk-to-reward ratio had changed, I would have to find a way to do the same for the product managers. I realized that I needed some leverage. Why not start at the top? I called Don Hall (as in the Hall family, which owns Hallmark). Actually, I called his secretary, who had absolutely no idea who I was. I told her I was setting up an important meeting to launch Hallmark into the gift business, and it was critical that Don Hall attend. She asked me when, and I asked her what would work for Mr. Hall's schedule. She gave me a date. I now had some serious leverage.

My next calls were to the other senior executives' offices. I explained to their secretaries that I was setting up a meeting to launch Hallmark into the gift business, but I wasn't sure if their bosses should attend; however, Don Hall would be there. Of course, they all thought their bosses should be there too. I now had a meeting scheduled with every senior executive throughout Hallmark Cards.

Then I wrote a letter to the product managers. I thanked them for all of their support and said that I was looking forward to seeing the products they had been developing. I also told them that if for any reason they couldn't deliver products again this year, they shouldn't worry: I had already set up a meeting to discuss the obstacles that were keeping Hallmark out of this multimillion-dollar market, and I attached a list of attendees. Thus, the Hallmark Gift Program was launched.

My passion overrode my fears, and I found the courage to act. I discovered a greater level of resourcefulness, confidence, and assertiveness within myself than I had ever dreamed existed. If I hadn't taken that risk, I'm not sure what would have happened. Chances are I wouldn't have been fired, but I would have been blamed and stripped of my pride. Because of that risk, I found the courage to follow a dream, to leave Hallmark, and go to work for Walt Disney.

Think of a time when you stood up for yourself, a time when you found an inner strength you didn't know existed. What did it feel like?

What were the strengths, talents, and passions that you tapped into? How did it change you?

If you find yourself with a challenge, a goal, or a dream that you want to follow but lack the courage, then look beyond the risks and rewards to uncover your fears and passions so that you can find the courage to act.

Consider:

What signature risks have helped define my life?

At the time, what were my fears behind taking those risks?

What passions did I have around my reward?

How did I find the courage I needed?

Invisible Risk

Playing It Too Safe

Great leaders are comfortable
being uncomfortable.

Identifying Hidden Risks

Some of you during the jump exercise in Chapter Four might have been thinking, "Hey, wait a minute! You changed the whole deal." I did. Chances are that initially you were thinking about what might happen to you if you took the risk. When I changed the scenario to include a loved one who was dying, chances are that your focus shifted to what would happen if you *didn't* take the risk. This allowed you to see the invisible risk involved in not acting.

Invisible risk is the risk of regret when we try to avoid risk and end up playing it too safe. It's often the regret of what might have been if we had pursued our talents, hopes, and dreams.

How About a Risk-Free Life?

At times, the challenges may seem too hard and you wish you could have a risk-free life. Some people say, "I'm not a risk taker. I want to avoid risk at all costs." Let's consider what kind of life that would be. How would that change your day?

Maybe now you jog around the block, take a shower, drink coffee, and make toast before driving to work. If you're going to avoid risk, you'd better cut out the jogging because you could twist your ankle. A lot of people fall in the shower, so don't go there. You might burn your tongue drinking coffee, so forget that. It's possible that you could shock yourself on the toaster or get in an accident on the road to work. Maybe you'd better just stay in bed. But you'd better not stay in bed: statistics show most people die lying in bed. Clearly there's no such thing as a risk-free life.

Let's look at the three most common types of invisible risk. I call them the Waiting Place, the Hiding Place, and the Ghosts of Risks Past.

The Waiting Place

Things that matter most must never be
at the mercy of things that matter least.
—Johann Wolfgang von Goethe

Failure to Act

It's easy to get caught up in the Waiting Place. It
happens when you find yourself wanting everything to be perfect, looking for a guarantee, wish-
ing it were easy, or thinking you don't have enough
time. However, when it comes to taking a risk,
you'll find that it's never perfect, there are no guarantees, it's seldom easy, and there is never enough
time or information.

A woman came up to me after one of my IntelligentRisking programs and confessed her need
for perfection. Suzanne had been waiting for an
assistant manager position to open up. By the
time the job became available, she wanted it desperately. Her goal was to send the perfect résumé
with impeccable references. She wanted to take
her time, so she thought she would write it over
the weekend. Before she submitted it, she wanted
a few of her close friends to review it. Then she
decided to print it on high-quality paper.

Still dissatisfied, she decided to redo it. Suzanne didn't want to send it out until she confirmed the exact title of the recipient. She wanted to deliver it in person and decided to wait until she bought a new suit so she'd look her best in case she ran into someone important. One month later, her résumé still wasn't ready. By the time she got it good enough, she learned the position had already been filled. Her need to be perfect cost her the perfect job.

No Risk

We live in a society that encourages risk taking. Our country and many of our most successful businesses were founded in risk; yet recently we have seen a proliferation of "risk-free" promotions. Have you ever actually tried to return one of those "no-risk," money-back items? If you still have the receipt and the original packing, plus lots of time, patience, and tenacity, then you may actually get your money back (if the offer hasn't already expired).

There are few guarantees in this life, and if anyone tells you that you can take a risk guaranteed to work, then you had better turn to someone else for advice.

The Time Is Now

It's never too late to start, and it's best not to put off until tomorrow things that matter today. If you catch yourself thinking, "That's something I'd love to try if I were just a little bit younger," then think again.

Olympic Moments of Opportunity

The Value of Time

To realize the value of one year,
ask a student who has failed a grade.

To realize the value of one month,
ask a mother who has given
birth to a premature baby.

To realize the value of one week,
ask an editor of a weekly newspaper.

To realize the value of one day,
ask the person who filed his taxes on April 16.

To realize the value of one minute,
ask the traveler who has just missed a plane.

To realize the value of one millisecond,
ask the athlete who just won a
silver medal at the Olympics.

—*Author unknown*

An Olympic Moment of Opportunity is that brief window of time when your mental, emotional, and physical readiness coincides with a situation that together offers you a high potential for success.

It's not every day that circumstances will call on your unique wisdom and experience. It's not every day that you feel fit and healthy. It's not every day you have the chance to help someone in trouble. It's not every day you can be a hero in your own adventure. Will you grab that once-in-a-lifetime opportunity and turn it into a once-in-a-lifetime success?

How to Break Out of the Waiting Place

If You Are a Perfectionist

- ✓ Set deadlines.
- ✓ Accept that everything won't go perfectly.
- ✓ Trust that you'll do your best.
- ✓ Don't grant yourself unlimited extensions to get more information.
- ✓ Make a decision, and take action.

If You Are Looking for a Guarantee

✓ Recognize there are no true guarantees.

✓ If you still feel you need a guarantee, then question if the risk is too high.

✓ Ask yourself if the guarantee is worth losing the opportunity over.

If You Want It Easier

✓ While you are waiting for a genie to come along and wave his magic wand, take one more step, then one more.

If You Are Waiting for More Time or the Right Time

Since no one has invented a way to make more time, try these ways to find the right time. When you hear yourself saying any of the following phrases (as you put off doing something that really matters), try a different approach. Change the way you think, and you'll change your life.

The Old Approach	*Positive Risk Approach*
I'll do it later.	I'll do it this week.
I'm too busy.	I'm simplifying my life.
I don't have the time.	If it's important, I'll find the time.
I have no time for myself.	I'm making time for myself.
I'll have time for this later.	What can I change to create time now?
My time just isn't my own.	I'm in charge of my time.
I'd love to, but I'm too busy.	Let's schedule it; I'll rearrange some things.

The Hiding Place

> I had a lot of troubles in my life
> but most of them never happened.
> —*Mark Twain*

Unwilling to Let Go

When you find your emphasis changing from "playing to win" to "playing not to lose," you know you have fallen into the Hiding Place. This invisible risk usually appears once you have achieved some measure of success. That's when we are more likely to shift from dynamic, proactive risk taking into a static, reactive mode. When we are content, we sometimes create boundaries, patterns, habits, rules, assumptions, and paradigms to protect us. The risk here is that we might end up trapped by our efforts to remain content.

The status quo is a moving target.

In lieu of seeking to fulfill a dream or pursue a passion, you decide that life isn't so bad in this comfort zone. You've got it made. Why rock the boat? You'll camp here. Are you making a temporary camp? Or is it looking a little more permanent? There are many examples of individuals who built and controlled empires, only to find that in their effort to protect what they had built, they had allowed their empires to control them. Then in an effort to protect his success, he allowed his empire to control him.

Change, a Critical Element

The longer you stand still, the further away you drift from your own desired goals. You don't have what you want, but you're afraid to move on, fearing that you'll lose what you do have.

Sometimes it's hard to accept that as hard as it is to let go and move forward, you must.

Entrepreneurial companies that catapult to success with cutting-edge products and services can grow conservative and timid as they attempt to retain their position. I joined Disney just after Walt Disney had passed away and there was a distinct void in the leadership. The entire company had slipped into a "if we change anything, we'll lose everything" mode.

No one dared to update the characters' looks. And when I reached across the table to point out where we might want to put Mickey Mouse on a skateboard, I thought I was going to have my hand slapped. The company had unknowingly slipped into a defensive posture to guard its position, forgetting the entrepreneurial strategies and skills it had used to garner success in the first place.

Fortunately, I reported indirectly to an outstanding leader, Bo Boyd. Bo has a unique style that blends common sense, vision, and political savvy. At the time, he was a vice president who later was promoted to president and then chairman of Disney Consumer Products. He has given me valuable counsel over the years and become a life-long friend. When I worked at Disney, I turned to him whenever I hit one of these invisible walls within the company. He gave me great advice that I continue to use to this day: "Barbara, always do the right thing, and ask for forgiveness later."

The company was facing an invisible risk: it was trying not to change in a world that was changing. What happened was that Michael Eisner arrived, with a takeover and a makeover that resulted in phenomenal success and growth.

How to Leave the Hiding Place

✓ Make sure you understand your fears.

✓ Make a list of what it is you are trying to protect.

✓ Add to your list how much all this protection is costing you in time, energy, and money.

✓ Challenge yourself by asking if you're spending more time, energy, and money worrying about doing it than it would take to actually do it.

✓ Make two more lists: a list of everything that you might actually lose and a list of everything you might realistically gain.

✓ Compare your lists, challenging each item for its validity. If you have more to lose than gain, you need to reconsider taking this risk.

✓ Ask yourself how you would feel if you quit.

✓ Ask yourself if you would have regrets.

✓ Consider the worst-case scenario, and then ask yourself if you could handle it. For example, rather than quit, perhaps you could find a way to take smaller steps, minimizing potential losses.

✓ Recognize that if you are putting most of your energy into trying not to lose, you are sabotaging your own efforts to win.

✓ Ask yourself if you are trying too hard to stay in your comfort zone.

✓ If you find yourself trapped in the status quo, find ways to break out.

The Ghosts of Risks Past

> Everyone thought I was bold and fearless and even arrogant, but inside I was always quaking.
> —*Katharine Hepburn*

The Ghosts of Risks Past are the memories of your own personal successes and failures. They can be a negative or a positive filter through which you view information and make judgments. These negative memories contribute to the voice of the monster within—that inner voice you hear when you begin to doubt yourself, your decisions, and your abilities. Your successful experiences create friendly ghosts that whisper encouragement, giving you the confidence to try again.

Women seldom overemphasize their successes; in fact, we do just the opposite: we tend to focus on and overemphasize our mistakes and failures. Sometimes your failures will haunt you to the point that they make your memories of an actual incident worse than the reality. Failures can promote excessive caution. A previous lack of success can contribute to your fears and persuade you to avoid risk at any cost. These ghosts provoke the monster within.

The Ghosts of Risks Past certainly play a role in how you filter information. They can blur your view, dominate your thoughts, and dictate your choices. Take a moment, and do a quick scan of your own ghosts. Are they encouraging or discouraging? If they are friendly, then you have a solid foundation. If the ghosts are frightening, then look at them in the light of positive risk to learn from past risks and to reframe failed attempts as nothing more than stepping-stones to future successes. In this way, you'll get back in control of them instead of them controlling you.

How to Tame the Ghosts of Risks Past

✓ Avoid thinking or saying, "I'm not good enough." Replace that phrase with, "I'm getting better every day."

✓ Take an inventory of your strengths and accomplishments. Keep that list handy and whenever possible, do things that play to your strengths.

✓ Build a strong support team that believes in you.

✓ If you're having a tough day, call someone on your team and tell him or her, "Today is hard; I need a pep talk."

✓ Tune out pessimists.

✓ Drop anyone who consistently tells you in a critical way that you aren't good enough.

✓ Pay attention to when you hear the monster within. Is it in the evenings? When you're tired? After arguing with family or friends? If you know when you're most likely to hear the monster, it will be easier for you to ignore its whispers.

✓ If the monster is breathing down your neck, get away. Break the mood and go to a movie, work out, read a book, or take a drive. Do something that makes you feel good and focuses your mind on something else.

✓ Look at the risk involved if you give up.

✓ Make a list of why you want to do this, and refer back to it when you question yourself.

✓ Visualize your future success. Whether you actually draw it, or create it out of words, or cut pictures out of magazines, create a picture of you reaching your goal, and keep it nearby. Pull it out anytime it gets hard to carry on.

What If?

If I try, I risk possible failure;
If I don't try, I risk certain failure.

If I change, I risk the unknown;
If I don't change, I risk being left behind.

If I believe in myself, I may risk disappointment;
If I don't believe in myself, I risk
not becoming all I can be.

If I climb, I risk falling;
If I don't climb, I risk never reaching the summit.

What If You Do?—What If You Don't?

Searching for invisible risks allows you to increase your information base and broaden your perspective. This enables you to make the best decision possible with the information you have available at the time. Invisible risks are dangerous only when we don't consider them in our decision-making process. Question yourself daily about your decisions, and examine how you filter information (subjective objectivity). As you climb your mountain, continue to ask every step of the way, "What if I do?" and "What if I don't?"

My friend Brian had the dramatic experience of being with others as they came to grips with their invisible risks during his twenty-plus years on the streets as a police officer and paramedic firefighter. He told me, "During this time, I had the opportunity to be with people in the final moments of their lives. Those were powerful, powerful moments."

The sad part was that so many people had regrets. Their regrets sounded like these: "I wish I had pursued that dream. I wish I had said the things I wanted to say to the people who meant the most to me. I wish I had taken a chance on the talent that was inside me. No one else knew it was there, yet I knew and I didn't take the chance." Not all of us have those feelings of regret, yet far too many of us do.

Regrets are insidious because the question of what might have been can haunt you forever. Regrets have a way of accumulating over the years. They can creep up on you and ambush you from behind long after you thought you had gotten over them. They subconsciously undermine your confidence and erode your spirit.

Run Away and Join the Circus!

I recently met Frank Felt, an extraordinary man. He has his Ph.D. in political science and was a senior analyst for the CIA. He was diagnosed with melanoma that had spread into his lymph nodes. His doctors removed his lymph glands and determined there was nothing else left to do. It was too late for chemotherapy. Their advice for him was to quit his job and do whatever would make him happy. He probably had only six months left to live, at the most a year.

Frank did just that. He quit his job, sold his house, bought a motor home, and went off to do something that he had only dreamed about since he was six years old: he ran off and joined the circus.

All of this happened to him twenty-four years ago, when he was forty-nine. Frank is now seventy-three, and he's still with the circus. He went from assistant manager to running the circus on the road to ringmaster, and today he is still managing the advanced sales. Amazing, isn't it?

I asked Frank, "With all your wisdom and twenty-twenty hindsight, what do you think happened?" He said, "I had been fascinated by the circus since my father took me at the age of five. When I got out of the service, it just didn't seem an appropriate choice for a career. How do you go home, and tell your family you're joining a circus? That diagnosis was a gift. It gave me the freedom to follow my dream. When I did join the circus, I never had to work so hard in my life, and I had never ever had so much fun. I just don't think I had time to be sick anymore."

What invisible risks are out there for you? Is there an area in your life in which you're playing it too safe? Is there something out there that you want to do but feel it would be safer if you didn't take the risk? Looking at risks from multiple perspectives is imperative. However, it is difficult for many of us to see the potential loss or negative consequence that comes with inaction. Too often we believe that if we do nothing, we'll be safe. We have the misconception that if we can just ignore what's happening around us, we won't have to take any risks at all.

Invisible Rewards

Just as there are invisible risks, there are invisible rewards that can be equally difficult to discern. If something doesn't turn out as you hoped, it is often hard to see the value in the experience. With positive risk, the invisible rewards are made up of the intangibles, like the confidence and pride you walk away with when you know you did the right thing for the right reason. Invisible rewards lie in the wisdom and insights you gain about yourself and how you will do things differently in the future. It is the depth of character and the empathy you acquire from the experience.

I once did an IntelligentRisking program for Peggy McAllister, executive director of the New Hampshire Association of School Principals. During the association's annual meeting, the members present the traditional Principal of the Year Award and also something special: Heroes in Education awards.

The year I was speaking at the conference, this honor was bestowed on a principal who had been pressured by his school board to fire one of his outstanding teachers. The reason they wanted this teacher let go was not for any substantial reason; rather, someone on the board had a personal conflict with the teacher.

The principal refused based on his principles, and he was subsequently relieved of his own job. He took the risk for the right reason: to protect a teacher from being wrongly dismissed. He deserved the Heroes in Education award. It would be great if every organization offered a "Hero" award to emphasize the need for and value of doing the right thing.

If you take the right risk for the right reason in the smartest way possible, even if it doesn't turn out as you hoped, it still usually turns out. In addition to several invisible rewards, the principal received a more tangible reward: a job in a different district that ended up being a better job, with more money and an opportunity for him to work with a school district that shared his values.

So often risks taken for the right reason that don't turn out quite the way we hope lead to greater opportunities and more tangible rewards down the road.

Consider:

Do I often find myself trying to play it too safe?

If I find myself waiting for everything to be perfect, how can I break out of the Waiting Place?

How will I prepare myself to act when my Olympic Moment of Opportunity comes along even if I don't feel ready?

If I find myself getting too comfortable, how will I nudge myself to try something new?

How will I replace the negative Ghosts of Risks Past with positive ghosts?

How will I train myself to look for the invisible risks I may face if I don't risk?

How will I find the invisible rewards in my situation?

Will I start asking myself, "What if I do?" and "What if I don't?"

6

IntelligentRisking

The IntelligentRisking Process

Life is either a daring adventure
or nothing at all.
—*Helen Keller*

The "How To"

Now that we have explored positive risk and its key components and concepts, it's time to move on from the "want to" to the "how to." Now the focus is on you. What are the challenges, goals, and dreams that you want to achieve? We'll look at how to choose the right goal, plan for it, and build your passion. We'll not only look at how to start but how to hang in there and see it through.

The Art of Simplicity

In this era of information overload, it's easy to make the simple complex, but the real trick is in making the complex simple. I feel that my job is to translate my thirty years of experience and ten years of research into a simple, practical, and useful guide with tools, strategies, and critical questions that you can put into action today. It took me one year to write this book and five years to simplify it. The beauty in the IntelligentRisking process is that it's simple enough to use as a quick reference and yet provides you with the ability to add the depth and complexity you need for serious challenges.

Taking risks can be a complicated and convoluted process. Depending on the risk, it can be easy to get caught up in the hundreds of things to consider and endless research and information that needs to be acquired. You may feel you need to speak with experts ranging from accountants to project managers and from bankers to futurists. However, the reality is that most of us have limited time and multiple priorities and few of us have the luxury of unlimited money and time to consider everything. What IntelligentRisking offers is a quick and straightforward way for you to evaluate your options.

Countless books have been written on the subject of risk management, but very few focus on personal leadership, women, and risk. The books I have found seem to be written from a man's point of view, and they lose me in a mass of background information, projections, and theories. I've searched for a book that would be relatively straightforward on the subject of risk—a book that would distill what I needed down into a manageable tool that would both remind me and help me to sort through some of the critical issues. Finding neither a book nor a process that fit the bill, I decided to develop my own.

IntelligentRisking: A Definition

IntelligentRisking (in tel' e jent risk ing) n. A positive, proactive process that will help you sort through which risks to take, determine the right timing, establish the best way to proceed, and draw on your passion to see it through.

IntelligentRisking focuses on your positive core, which will increase your probability for achievement by helping you maximize the odds for success while reducing the odds for a loss. IntelligentRisking is not a mysterious talent that some have and some don't; it's a real-world approach that appeals to your common sense. It's an art that's developed over a lifetime.

IntelligentRisking has these elements:

Astuteness	Premeditation
Confidence	Intuition
Awareness	Optimism
Courage	Proaction
Determination	Resourcefulness
Thoughtfulness	Commitment
Positive attitude	Assertiveness
Purposefulness	Information and inspiration
Wisdom	

Information, Inspiration, and Action

Even if you're on the right track, you'll get run over if you just sit there.
—*Will Rogers*

IntelligentRisking blends information and inspiration. Have you ever wanted to lose ten pounds? Most of us have. Unless you have a rare medical condition, there are only two ways to lose weight: eat less or exercise more or, better yet, do both. We all know it isn't the information that we're missing that keeps us from losing weight. It's the inspiration. That's why there are at least one hundred diet books on bookstore shelves at any given time. Why? We want to hear that there is an easy way.

Some of my personal favorites are *How to Eat Everything You Want and Still Lose Weight* and *How to Look Great Without Exercising.* The reality is that you can have all the information and inspiration in the world, but unless you act, nothing will change.

The same is true with risk. There is so much information out there today that whether you decide to take the risk or not, you can find enough data to prove you are right. So it's often not the information that helps us decide our course of action; it's the inspiration. Choosing to take a risk usually comes down to your passion: how much you want to achieve your goal. The information is what allows you to be smart about it. Yet the key is still in taking action.

Mountain Analogy

> Climbing Mt. Everest is basically a
> challenge between the individual and
> themselves and the individual and their
> mountain. In life, we are all climbing
> a mountain like Everest and the key to
> success is much the same. It's not the
> mountain we conquer, it's ourselves.
> —*Sir Edmund Hillary*

Using a mountain analogy can make a valuable shift in your perspective about risk. This in turn will help you internalize your own challenges in a new way, creating a powerful visual parallel to your own goals. You will find that you can simplify things professionally or personally by asking questions such as, "What is the real mountain here?" and "What mountain am I climbing?"

The most important climb is the one you are on at the moment. Doing well on this mountain is what will determine your forward progress. There will always be others who take more difficult routes or climb more dangerous mountains. Your focus can't be on them. At any time, you may be able to look backward or forward and see other mountains that may seem more or less important in comparison. Yet the mountain you are climbing today is the only one that truly matters now.

When climbing a technical route on an actual mountain, you climb one pitch (or rope length) at a time. The bigger the mountain is, the more pitches are required. The truth is that if you can climb one pitch, you can climb a mountain. The same is true for the mountains you face in your own life.

IntelligentRisking Strategies

Each of us faces challenges and goals
with associated risks. They are the
mountains we must climb.

In an effort to help you simplify and clarify your own risk-taking process, we will be looking at the four simple strategies that IntelligentRisking is built on:

  I. Choose your mountain

 II. Plan your route

III. Build your courage

IV. Climb strong!

Although there are many questions to ask, each strategy is divided into the critical questions key to that specific strategy. These questions are the ones that every woman needs to ask herself before she risks. Refer to Appendix A to review the Positive Risk Checklist, which provides a complete list of the fifteen Critical IntelligentRisking questions.

7

Strategy I: Choose Your Mountain

Many of you have faced bigger challenges and taken greater risks than I have. It's important to me that you know that I respect and honor all of you and the mountains you have climbed.

Critical Question #1
What's My Mountain?

The mountains you chose yesterday
have defined who you are today.
The mountains you choose today will
define who you will become tomorrow.

The first decision any climber must make is to choose which mountain to climb.

Creating a Compelling Future

We are all climbing a mountain in our lives, some literally and some figuratively. Having a clear goal creates a certain amount of synergy, which translates into a tremendous level of focused energy. In truth, the challenge you decide to pursue creates a compelling future. It starts to define your choices and actions.

George Burns set his sights on performing in the London Palladium to celebrate his hundredth birthday. The theater had even sold tickets to the show. Although he didn't get to perform there on that date, he did celebrate his one-hundredth birthday. He died forty-three days after he reached his goal. How did he live so long? I believe it is because he had created a clear and compelling future for himself.

Focus

You get what you focus on. If you choose to become a world-class ballet dancer, you may or may not achieve your goal of being one of the best, yet somewhere during the pursuit of that goal, you will become a ballet dancer. The key is to choose.

If I asked you not to think about a yellow-spotted purple dragon, what would you think about? Imagine that you were just told you are going to compete in the next Olympics, which begins twelve months from today. You must compete; however, you can choose which event. In fact, you have a guaranteed spot on the team. Which event would you choose? How would your focus change? How would you train? What else in your life would change? Imagine this same effect created with any mountain.

Choosing which mountain to climb is one of the most important decisions you'll make because it determines what direction you'll take in your life. What does your mountain look like? You may be thinking of changing jobs or starting your own business. Perhaps you're struggling with an illness or facing problems in a relationship. Maybe you long to rediscover the hidden athlete inside yourself. In quiet moments, you may hear the beckoning whispers from a lost dream or hidden talent. Remember Frank Felt, and take the time to look for the right mountain. It can change your life.

Intangible Energy

When you choose your mountain, you set a path and create a magnetic power that helps draw you toward your goal. You'll start finding the information, people, and energy you'll need to climb. Once you are clear on your goal and committed to it, you'll be amazed at how events start shaping themselves.

Remember the last time the thought of buying a car went through your mind? Probably your first thought was, "No, I don't really need a new car; the one I have is fine." Then you made some kind of decision: you may have dismissed the idea and went in a different direction, or you may have started down the path of justifying how you really did need a new car. If you went down this second path, you began to notice car ads on television and in newspapers and magazines. Yesterday you hadn't even seen them, yet today they seem to be everywhere. You find yourself talking to friends about their cars. You stop by a dealership to look. You find a car that is really cool, and you think to yourself that this car is special and there aren't many out there like it. Then the salesperson offers you an incredible deal that you can't pass up. Now you own a new car. You drive it off the showroom floor, and then everywhere you look, there are cars just like it. Hmmm . . .

There is an incredible amount of intangible but powerful energy that you tap into when you are climbing the right mountain. It creates a positive force in your life that will help keep other kinds of negativity at bay. I'm sure you've experienced it. You get so wrapped up and involved in a project that your passion around it almost creates a shield that wards off negativity.

Four Ways to Find Your Mountain

There are basically four ways we find mountains:

1. We choose freely.
2. Someone chooses for us.
3. We find one by default.
4. Life hands us a mountain.

With free choice, you may decide to do what Frank Felt did: quit your job and join the circus. Of course, until Frank truly chose his own mountain, he was climbing someone else's. If someone else is choosing your mountain for you, then you might find yourself in a position like the accountant who is so good at handling difficult clients that management decides to transfer her into sales.

Consider this scenario: there is an opening in the regional office in San Francisco, where you've always wanted to live. It's the position you've wanted for a long time, and you know you'd be perfect for it. You have the experience and the qualifications. In fact, your boss told you the job was yours if you wanted it. It's just that you never got around to sending in that résumé. Now you've been transferred and are seeing clients in Timbuktu. You might say you didn't choose that mountain, yet in truth you chose it by default.

And then there will be that time when life hands you a mountain. We'll all get one like this some day. The phone will ring, and it will be that call you hoped you'd never get. Now you have a new mountain to climb.

Mount Everest Is Not the Tallest Mountain

Every personal mountain has an impact on us professionally, and every professional mountain has an impact on us personally. Sometimes people are hesitant to choose a mountain because they want the "perfect" mountain or they feel as if theirs isn't important or large enough.

There is a general misconception that the right mountain can be found only by free choice. That's not always true. It doesn't matter how you find your mountain. Sometimes it doesn't even matter if you like the mountain. That was certainly the case with my best friend, Valari. She has been diagnosed with cancer six times over the past ten years. This was a series of mountains that life handed her. Valari's choice wasn't which mountain or if she'd climb. Her choice was how she would climb.

She claimed those mountains with passion and chose to climb them with strength, courage, and determination. She did not back down from the challenge or hand this burden to anyone else. She got involved, did her research, called all the shots, picked the route, climbed each pitch, and took the risks one at a time. Not only did she not back down; Valari did her fair share of handing out mountains to others, particularly her doctors. I can confirm the rumor that they snapped to attention when she entered a room—not out of fear but out of their sheer respect and admiration for her. Valari's focus and attention to her mountain was rewarded by enjoying a wonderfully full life.

In reality, it doesn't matter how you come across your mountain. Choosing it may not be any better in the long run than one you stumble across by accident. The best mountains are those you discover a passion around, no matter how it comes to you.

Interestingly, it does not seem to be the size of the goal that matters as much as its clarity and its significance to you. Our lives are made up of many different chapters. Although you may not have found them yet, there will be chapters in your life that will feel as if you're climbing Mount Everest. And there will be other chapters that seem much easier in comparison. It is important not to feel your mountain isn't valuable because it isn't huge. In fact, just the opposite is true: enjoy and learn from these fun, easy climbs while you can. Together all of these chapters make up a full life.

It Doesn't Matter How You Find Your Mountain

People have different ways of finding their mountains. Some just know. Others need to explore before they find the right one. And still others end up with the right mountain out of default.

What matters the most is that you find the right mountain, not how you find it.

Nancy, Cami, and Retta are all climbing the same mountain; they are all attorneys at Jackson Walker. Yet they found their mountain in very different ways. Nancy Hamilton walked away from her mountain, yet found it being handed back to her by life.

Cami Boyd just knew her mountain. She was nine years old and sitting with her father in a Chinese restaurant when he asked her what she thought she'd like to do when she grew up. Although she was only in the fourth grade, she was certain she wanted to be an attorney. Cami remembers how surprised he was at her answer, given that there were no attorneys in the family. She has never wavered from her goal. Cami graduated from Syracuse University and is now a nationally respected commercial litigator and a partner in the Jackson Walker law firm in Dallas, Texas, with expertise in intellectual property, trademark, and copyright law.

Retta Miller is also a top trial attorney and partner at Jackson Walker. She specializes in litigation and arbitration involving securities, intellectual property, and business disputes. You might think that to achieve this level of success, Retta must have always known that her mountain would be law, yet law wasn't her first career.

Retta started out her professional life with a degree in home economics from Oklahoma State University in 1975. It was only after several years in that field that she realized the career she had chosen wasn't right for her. In her own words, "It just didn't float my boat." Still undecided about what other career she wanted to pursue, she took some aptitude tests and discovered she might make an excellent attorney. Although she took her admissions test and applied to law school at the last possible moment, everything fell into place. Within twelve weeks, she found herself accepted by Northwestern University Law School.

Retta found the right mountain—one that tapped into her passion. The rest is history. When she was graduating from Northwestern, she received a number of job offers and decided to accept a position with Jackson Walker. It is a decision that Retta, now a partner, has never regretted.

Consider the Possibilities

As you consider your possibilities, think about improbable things. Sometimes the choices we make may sound crazy, if not impossible, to others but are in fact grounded in sound ideas, goals, and commitment. Jenny and Jimmy Desmond are an example of stepping out of the box. Once this young couple graduated from college, they married and left with their backpacks to tour the world. Their passion for animal rights directed their travels and led them to opportunities beyond their wildest dreams. They worked with chimpanzees in Uganda and orangutans in Borneo. They lived in a tree house in the forests of Africa and learned to track wildlife by foot in Zimbabwe. They also did much less glamorous, but no less valuable, work, like working in Sydney as a nanny and a tree surgeon. They also picked fruit and lived in a trailer park while working at a lobster factory.

Their travels around the world on their honeymoon lasted several years and eventually led them back to Boston. To legitimize their commitment to protecting animals and wildlife worldwide, Jimmy is now in vet school and Jenny has started her own studio photographing animals. Some may think that their return to the states was a much safer and conventional choice. To them, their decision to go back to school and start a business seemed radical because it was so conventional. They felt it was a risk to give up a life they knew and loved for a more conservative path. However, they are comfortable with their choice because they are betting on the fact that this new route will help them climb their true mountain and achieve their greater dream of working for animal conservation.

It's time to claim your own mountain, big or small. All that really counts is that it's a mountain you believe in. At this point, there are usually three reactions I get from people: some know exactly what their mountain is, some have so many mountains that it's difficult to narrow it down to just one, and some others still aren't sure that they have a real mountain.

If you already know your mountain, I want you to challenge yourself to make sure this is the right mountain for you. If you have too many mountains—and most women do—then as you read, try to prioritize them and (for the sake of learning) focus on just one for right now. The information we'll explore will help you clarify your choices. Or you may have had a clear mountain but now find yourself unsure of what mountain you really want to climb next. All of us find ourselves in this position at some time. If you aren't sure, then going through the following exercise will help you find your mountain.

Possibility Lists

Make a list of all the things that are of interest to you, even if they seem wild, crazy, or unconventional. Then explore them to see what sparks your passion. In fact, ask some friends what they think your passions are. Then go alone or drag a friend to a new event, show, play, or activity once a month until you find something that grabs you. Don't just stay on the straight-and-narrow path; explore some of those forbidden areas that you've always been curious about.

There are a number of areas to consider for possibility lists—for example:

✓ Interests, passions, and hobbies

✓ Personal strengths and weaknesses

✓ Organizations that you find interesting

✓ Things that are dear to you

✓ Experiences when you lost complete track of time

✓ Things you love to do that don't cost much

✓ Things you used to love doing but don't have
  time for anymore

✓ What you wanted to be when you grew up

✓ Services you would enjoy doing for others

✓ Your favorite daydreams

✓ Areas of curiosity

If you run short on ideas, visit your local bookstore or library, or perhaps look through the Yellow Pages. If you intend to make a list and then choose from it, make sure that you put together some great lists, because the idea you choose can never be better than the ideas on that list. An invisible risk would be to limit the possibilities you consider. Don't allow yourself, knowingly or unknowingly, to start listening or believing or living within the limitations others have placed on you. Consider all the possibilities, especially the outrageous ones.

Mind Map

If you aren't a list person, you might want to try mind-mapping your ideas. Start with a central theme, and branch out from there—for example:

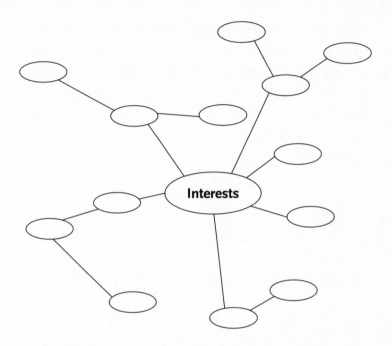

You can have subgroups of subgroups of subgroups. The only limits are the ones you impose.

The Why

As you consider your choices, a key question to consider is, "Why?" What is it about this mountain that grabs you? What passion does it tap into for you?

One way to understand whether this really is your mountain is to figure out how much passion you have for it. What are your own personal reasons for climbing this mountain? What is it about this mountain that fires you up? What is the attraction? What is it about this one that gives you motivation? To ensure this is the right mountain, ask yourself the following questions:

✓ *Does it create a compelling future for you?* Do you find yourself thinking about your goal all the time? Do you dream about it? Are you constantly talking to others about it? If you accomplish it, will it draw you closer to being the kind of person you'd like to be?

✓ *Is it a worthy goal?* Is this mountain worthy of your effort, time, and resources? Will climbing this mountain create something good for you or others? (By the way, I certainly consider climbing for the pure fun, enjoyment, and exhilaration a worthy goal.)

Understanding Your Mountain

To be sure it is all you hope it will be, it's important to take the time to get to know your mountain well once you've zeroed in on what you'll need to learn as much as possible about it. This will help you understand more about your "why." Turn to books, articles, the Web, and others who are involved so that you go beyond a superficial look and learn about the realities of your goal.

Sometimes people pick a mountain that sounds attractive, but once they start the climb, they realize it's not anything close to what they had expected. Can you remember the day when you couldn't wait to have the job you have right now? The one that is driving you nuts? Remember waiting for the phone to ring hoping that you'd be offered this job? Remember thinking how everything would fall into place if only you could get this job? Remember how nice your supervisors were to you when they interviewed you? Perhaps they even took you out to lunch, and you haven't had time for lunch since you took this job.

My second son, Nick, decided last year to look for a job. He landed an interview but misunderstood the time and arrived exactly thirty minutes late. They did not have time to squeeze him in, so they reluctantly agreed he could come back to interview the next day. This time he arrived thirty minutes early and quite nervous. When he arrived, they informed him that they had decided not to interview him after all. He was crestfallen. Then they added that the reason they weren't going to interview him for the job was that his résumé was so strong that they had decided to forgo the process and simply hire him. He was thrilled.

When he got home, he shared his story. I asked him what he was going to be doing. His answer was, "Darn! That was one thing I wanted to ask, but I forgot." Then I asked him how much they were going to pay him. Again, his answer was, "Darn! That was the other thing I really wanted to ask, but I forgot."

Being that excited about a job when you have no idea what you have to do or how much you'll get paid is a gift of innocence and a once-in-a-lifetime experience. It was refreshing to see him so thrilled to get his first job, even if he had no idea what mountain he was on. Yet within six months, it became crystal clear to Nick that this was not a job he wanted. Was it a valuable experience? Absolutely. He learned a tremendous amount about what it was he liked and disliked that he could never have figured out sitting at home.

At age sixteen, having no clue as to what you want tends to sort itself out. The more things you try, the more you zero in on what it is you want to do with your life. This lesson is valid throughout our lives. The more you experience, the more you discover about yourself.

However, it's critical to understand your mountain before you start to climb if it's of the Mount Everest variety. In fact you may want to consider an internship. Try the mountain on for size before you buy. You certainly don't want to spend the time and money to become a veterinarian only to find out after you open your own practice that you don't like animals. (You may laugh at this, but it does happen.)

Leslie Carlson provides a great example of how to choose your own mountain as she explores her options with the Garden of the Gods Club. It is an exclusive private property in Colorado Springs, Colorado, originally developed by H. L. Hunt's daughter, Margaret, and her husband, Al Hill, as a summer retreat for family and friends. Several years ago, the Garden of the Gods' club administrators decided to bring in Destination Hotels and Resorts, a leading professional property management company, to develop opportunities for the club. The original general manager who took on this project was so successful that he was promoted and moved to another property.

The club, now owned by Hunt Petroleum, was looking for a general manager to handle this premier family property. As the search went on, Leslie Carlson, vice president of operations for DH&R, stepped in to handle the transition. Although several candidates were presented, the expectations were high, and none of them quite fit the bill. In the meantime, Leslie became immersed in the details of this complex property and learned the business. At the same time, the Hunt family members still involved with the club were getting comfortable with Leslie running the show. In fact, they were so impressed with her that they asked if she was interested in taking over as the general manager.

As much as she loved working with the club, Leslie declined. She enjoyed working with a variety of properties, she didn't want to give up her strategic corporate role, and she wasn't sure Hunt Petroleum was willing to give her the autonomy she would need to develop the property. However, she stayed on at the club as the search for the general manager continued. Four months later, Hunt Petroleum came to her and basically said, "Tell us what it would take to make you stay." By now Leslie had been on a long enough "internship" that she knew this was a career change she wanted to make—*if* she could retain her strategic corporate role and *if* she was given the power and authority to make the necessary changes to develop the business. Everyone said, "Yes!" Leslie retained her corporate vice presidency and became the new general manager at the Garden of the Gods Club.

It was only through Leslie's "internship" that she was able to gather the information and the inspiration she needed to make this significant change in her life. Months later, she is confident that she took the right risk in the smartest way possible. It would have been a mistake to accept the position the first time. By waiting, she was able to take this job on her own terms, which in the end was the best for everyone involved.

Trust Your Intuition

Have you ever believed in an idea that everyone else thought was crazy? J. Madden, a successful real estate developer in the Denver area, thought it would be a great idea to build an upscale athletic club in the Denver Tech Center, an area of Denver that was being developed as a premier upscale office location for up and coming high-tech companies. He wanted this to be a smart risk, so he hired a consultant to research and evaluate the viability of his concept. The facts were gathered. The information led the consultant to conclude that it was not a good idea.

But this information didn't match Madden's intuition. His instinct told him it would work. To go ahead with his idea in the face of this research would be a significant risk. Madden struggled with trying to balance the quantitative analysis with the qualitative feeling that he believed in his heart. His passion and trust in his own instincts provided his "why."

He modified his plans, changed his route slightly, and then made his crux move by building the Greenwood Athletic Club. Ten years later, it is one of the most successful health clubs in the country. He proved that success means blending information with inspiration: listening to your intuition and then taking dynamic action.

If You're Still Looking for a Mountain

If you're still unsure of your mountain, it could be for a variety of reasons. You may have just finished a climb and are not quite ready for the next mountain. Perhaps you realize that you have been climbing someone else's mountain for so long that you are now searching for your own. Or maybe you aren't satisfied with the mountains you're climbing and are looking for a new mountain that would be more meaningful.

Without any mountain in your life, it is easy to drift away from the person you want to be. So if you feel you aren't sure of a mountain, consider making "finding your mountain" your mountain. It will prove to be an enlightening and interesting journey.

Your Response to Critical Question #1: What's My Mountain?

It's time to choose your mountain. After you have looked at and reviewed all of the possibilities and you're clear on the "why," decide on the goal, challenge, or dream that you want to pursue.

Critical Question #2
Whose Mountain Is It?

If you aren't choosing your
own risks, someone else will
be choosing them for you.

Every one of us has woken up one day only to discover that we've been climbing someone else's mountain.

The Real Mountain

It was Chris's first day in kindergarten. When Mrs. Smith announced, "Today we are going to draw a picture," Chris started drawing right away. Then Mrs. Smith said, "Stop, we aren't ready to begin yet." Chris thought, *What do you mean? I'm ready!*

Mrs. Smith then said, "Today we are going to draw a flower." Chris right away started drawing a black dragon flower that breathed fire. Mrs. Smith was walking along all the desks and looked at Chris's drawing. She said, "Don't you know how to draw a flower? I'll show you." And she drew a red flower with a green stem.

Chris looked at Mrs. Smith's flower. It was an okay flower, but he liked his flower better. He looked around the room and saw that everyone else was drawing flowers like Mrs. Smith's. He didn't want to get into any trouble on the first day of kindergarten, so he turned his page over and started drawing a red flower just like Mrs. Smith's. When Mrs. Smith came by again she stopped, smiled, and congratulated Chris: "You are a wonderful artist. Your flower looks just like mine."

Fortunately all of the kindergarten teachers I know are just the opposite of the teacher depicted above. However, I believe that many of us have had experiences over the course of our lifetimes that are similar to the one I just described. I use this story because it provides a painfully clear example of how life and the people around us, sometimes with the best of intentions, can sometimes pressure us to conform to an unwritten norm. It can be easy for any one of us to lose our way and begin to adopt someone else's beliefs and standards as our own.

You might be thinking that the mountain you have chosen is not really your mountain—but someone else's; however, you still find you want to climb it. Maybe the mountain belongs to your boss, your husband, your children, or your best friend. If you seriously challenge yourself and still find that you want to climb someone else's mountain, then perhaps you are actually climbing a different mountain altogether. Maybe the real mountain is having a relationship, keeping your job, or getting a promotion. It may not be that you are climbing someone else's mountain. It may actually be just a route you are taking to achieve your own goal. It's critical that you are crystal clear on the real mountain.

Believing in Your Mountain

If you don't believe in the mountain (or your organization doesn't), then it will be very difficult to climb it successfully. I was asked to help start up a new division of Mattel Toys called Emotions. Our goal was to develop and sell toy-like products into gift channels of distribution. We weren't meeting with a lot of success, so we had this brainstorm: What if our parent company, Mattel Toys, gave us the rights to make a porcelain Barbie doll?

It's important to understand that at Mattel, Barbie is untouchable. No one messes with her. We asked for permission anyway and to our astonishment were told, "Fine. However, you're on your own." We should have known something was up, yet you know that saying: Never look a gift horse in the mouth.

Our team didn't know the first thing about how to make a porcelain doll or dress it. I remember getting into my car and driving around to fabric shops in Beverly Hills looking for the right material to create the perfect outfit for our first porcelain Barbie. It turned out there weren't many fabric shops in Beverly Hills. I guess there isn't a lot of sewing or craft work happening in that part of town. Next, I was on airplanes traveling all over the world, trying to set up vendor networks. We found a gifted Russian sculptor, Igor Kunnonav, who made the original sculpture. Then I took the bullet train into the middle of Japan to work with older Japanese gentlemen who were among the best at porcelain casting and hand painting.

Some months later, our prototype Porcelain Barbie was done. We took her to Mattel for approval, and everyone was shocked. It turned out that Mattel had tried for years to make a Barbie out of porcelain. However, the company had determined that with her delicate fingers and toes, she was impossible to replicate out of porcelain.

So why was it that Mattel Toys, with vast worldwide resources, couldn't make a Porcelain Barbie when a tiny, untrained team at a small subsidiary could? Mattel simply didn't believe in the mountain. And it didn't have to: it was already successful with its existing line of Barbie plastic dolls. We, however, went after the development of a porcelain Barbie as if the world depended on it.

This is proof positive of the old adage: It's not the dog in the fight, it's the fight in the dog.

Committing to Your Mountain

There's a big difference between making a commitment and having a strong interest. Whether you are thinking about walking every day, losing ten pounds, or changing jobs, not much will happen with only a casual interest. Now that you have narrowed down your list, you should be clear on your mountain, why you're climbing it, and how you define success. Now it's time to commit.

I once did a program for Lincoln/Mercury, and the top executive there decided to share his mountain and his route with his entire team. This very successful businessman was quite comfortable with both professional and physical risk taking. His mountain was one he had wanted to climb for years, yet with each passing day, he found it more and more difficult to tackle: telling his parents he loved them. He shared with his team his goal and that his plan was to do this during his family reunion taking place in three weeks.

Why do you think he was willing to share such a personal mountain with his team? One thing was certain: he gained a tremendous amount of respect from his team for having the courage to share his goal with them. I don't believe that this man was having a "soft" moment. I think he passionately cared about this mountain and knew that by sharing it, he was virtually guaranteeing his own success. There wasn't any way he would want to come back from his vacation and have to tell one hundred people that he had backed down again. He wrote me a letter the week he returned, proud that he had reached his summit.

Declaring Your Mountain

There is power in declaring your mountain to others. Once you've committed to yourself, start telling others of your goal to help ensure your own success. It's odd that we are often more willing to break a deal with ourselves than we are willing to go back on a goal that we've shared with others.

Your Response to Critical Question #2: Whose Mountain Is It?

Now it's time for you to decide if this is truly your mountain. If it is, then you need to commit to it by declaring it to yourself and telling others about your goal.

Critical Question #3
How Do I Define Success?

*Choose a mountain to climb, and
you'll find the talents to climb it.*

To find meaningful success requires that you define success based on your own individual preferences. Although this can be a difficult task, defining success clearly by your own standards will make it easier to achieve.

Summit Fever

The single greatest loss of life on Mount Everest in history occurred in 1996 because so many climbers defined success as getting to the summit at all costs. This is called *summit fever,* and with that definition of success, people can make some bad choices.

When Sir Edmund Hillary was asked how he would feel if it were proven that George Mallory had actually reached the summit of Mount Everest first, Hillary replied, "I personally have found it equally important to get back down the mountain alive." It's important to be on guard against summit fever with your own mountain and to avoid the temptation to reach your goal at any cost to yourself or others.

Understanding Success

It's critical that you understand the balance required for you to be happy, or you may end up with a hollow victory. Most of us, if we were willing to set aside everything else in our lives and focus every ounce of our strength, energy, and thought into achieving a single goal, would probably achieve success.

However, would giving up everything be worth it? What if there was no one to share it with? What if it meant losing health or emotional stability? The Centers for Disease Control and Prevention recently released statistics indicating that 80 percent of every health care dollar spent in this country is related to stress.[1] Sometimes I think we spend our youth for wealth and then our wealth for health.

How would you define success if you were running a marathon? What if you won the race but pushed yourself so hard you were never able to run again? What if you didn't win the race but you finished it when others thought you didn't have it in you? What if you ran the race and didn't finish because of a twisted ankle, yet you became best friends with the medic who helped you? Who won?

Success Components

To help you define success on your own terms, I have listed a number of categories to start your thought process. Although these are a good place to start, it's important to customize this list to fit your own needs, so add any other categories or subcategories that you think would be of benefit to you.

It's critical to be clear on how you define success because the route you plan in Chapter Eight will be based on your definition of success. If you define success by simply making it to the summit of Mount Everest, then you won't need to pack extra oxygen tanks for getting back down. I've found that there are essentially six components that cover most of the bases. Consider how you might define success for your mountain as it relates to these categories (feel free to add more categories):

✓ Professional

✓ Personal

✓ Financial

✓ Emotional

✓ Physical

✓ Spiritual

How do you define success for your mountain? What prescription would you write for yourself? Perhaps thinking of it as a recipe will help. Most recipes for cookies, for example, share some common ingredients, such as flour, sugar, and eggs. Yet each recipe has its own unique ingredients and approach that creates its own end result. Adding chocolate chips will taste quite different from adding raisins. Eating the batter versus baking the cookies for ten minutes versus forgetting about them and baking them for thirty minutes will certainly give the final consumer a different flavor.

You may start out using two cups of one ingredient, a teaspoon of another, and just a dash of spice to give it pizzazz. As you grow and change over time, so will your taste, and the recipe will need to be adjusted. Following are some lists of sample questions to help you start thinking about what your own personal recipe might look like.

Professional

✓ What type of job?

✓ What type of organization?

✓ What hours?

✓ What days of the week do you work?

✓ How are you paid: salary, commission, or bonus?

✓ How are you evaluated?

✓ How challenging do you want the work to be?

✓ Do you work on a team or alone?

✓ Who do you work for?

✓ What title do you want?

✓ Are there additional perks?

Personal

✓ How much free time do you have?

✓ Where do you want to live?

✓ How close do you want to be to family and
friends?

✓ Do you have a good support group?

✓ Do you have access to the activities
you love?

✓ Are you involved in healthy relationships?

✓ Do you have children?

✓ Is there time for you?

✓ Do you spend quality time with those you're
close to?

Financial

✓ How much money do want to make?

✓ How much money will you be happy making?

✓ What kind of house do you need or want?

✓ How many cars do you want or need?

✓ Do you have enough money beyond your
house payment to enjoy life?

✓ Do you have enough savings in case something happens?

✓ Are you saving enough for your retirement?

✓ Is money how you measure success?

Emotional

✓ How often do you laugh?

✓ How much stress can you handle?

✓ How do you relax?

✓ Do you ever relax?

✓ Do you have time to play?

✓ How do you play?

✓ Do you feel satisfied at the end of the day?

✓ How well do you get along with others?

✓ Do you feel emotionally resilient?

✓ Do you take time out for yourself?

Physical

✓ Are you healthy?

✓ Are you fit and strong?

✓ Do you work out regularly?

✓ Are you eating well?

✓ Do you get the sleep you need?

✓ Do you feel rested?

✓ Do you have a great network of doctors?

Spiritual

✓ Are you at peace with your soul?

✓ Are you finding ways to help others?

Redefining Success

Success can be defined in many different ways. Odyssey of the Mind is a program designed to encourage creative problem solving and risk taking in children. The project one year was to create a device that would move across water. All the teams except one came up with some great yet traditional approaches to solve the problem. The other team's idea was highly unusual: they decided to try to duplicate the way a water spider (the *Renata fusca*) moves across a lake. They designed a device that would recreate the same type of tension on the water surface as this spider.

Their device failed. In fact, it sank during the competition; however, the judges agreed it was by far the most ingenious idea they had ever seen at the contest. Even though the idea failed, the judges knew that they had to reward that team's creativity to send the right message. They were also wise enough to realize that if the only thing they rewarded was success, they would be teaching the children to submit only ideas that would work rather than pursuing their best ideas. It would all but guarantee that every team would start thinking in terms of not failing rather than winning.

The judges in their wisdom challenged their definition of success and decided to broaden it. They created a whole new award, the Renata Fusca, which holds an esteemed and special place in the competition. It is one of the few awards not given yearly. Instead, it is saved and given to those persons or teams that exhibit exceptional creativity and innovation.

Challenging Your Definition

If your definition of success is found in only one category, then you may want to reconsider it. As far as risk goes, every parent, every individual, and every organization wants others to take risks as long as they can guarantee they'll work. However, this type of attitude is stifling and sends one message: it is okay to take risks that you guarantee will work. This defeats the entire premise of risk taking because there is no option for an unexpected outcome. Yet it is our failures that create unexpected outcomes and provide us, individually and collectively, with giant leaps in performance and development.

If you want to make a change in your own risk-taking ability or in that of those on your team, then you might want to consider rewarding risks that didn't work as long as they were on target strategically and tackled in a smart way. I'm not suggesting that you reward wild shots or dumb chances. A smart risk is one that has go/no-go criteria built in so that losses can be contained. However, if you begin rewarding risks that don't turn out as planned yet have all the elements of a Renata Fusca, you'll start sending a new message: "I want to take smart, strategic risks."

Definitions Are Dynamic

Now that you have defined success for yourself, it's critical that you remain open-minded. As you start to climb your mountain, your situation may change, so it's important that how you define success is not written in stone. What works today may not work tomorrow. Your definition will continue to evolve and change as you evolve and grow.

Your Response to Critical Question #3: How Do I Define Success?

Now it's time for you to create your own definition of success. Take a moment and jot down how you need to blend all the ingredients (professional, personal, financial, emotional, physical, and spiritual) into your own unique formula for success.

8

Strategy II: Plan Your Route

Now that you have chosen your mountain, it's time to look at creating a plan for climbing it. This plan will capitalize on your positive core as well as be flexible and dynamic.

Critical Question #4
What's My Route?

Choose a mountain, and the
future starts organizing it.

Positive Core

For every mountain, there are hundreds, if not thousands, of possible routes. Every mountain requires a different plan of approach based on who's climbing and how that person defines success. The key is to create a route that will capitalize on your own unique positive core, which is based on your own strengths, talents, and passions. This requires both objective and subjective information.

As an example, traditional project management may determine that the best plan for going back to school (for a person who is working full time and on a tight budget) would be for that person to continue working and pick up one or two courses every semester until he or she finishes the degree. This might be the perfect solution for some people. This route would appeal to them because it fits their personality. For many others, that plan would limit their chances for success. Based on their personalities, the right route would be quite different. They would be better off quitting their jobs, getting a student loan, and taking extra credits to finish school as quickly as possible. This route may work better because they would see it as a way to keep up their passion, get a better job sooner, pay off the loan faster, and move on to the next mountain.

The best route is the one that builds off your positive core and matches how you define success while blending qualitative and quantitative information.

Defining Your Positive Core

To begin defining your positive core, think of times when you felt you were performing at your peak. What allowed you to reach that level? Make a list of the strengths, talents, and passions you were using. What is it that your friends say you're good at? Add that to the list. What are you doing when you lose track of time? Add that to the list.

Make your list as long as possible, adding to it from some of the exercises you've already done in this book. It doesn't have to be formal, lengthy, or professionally put together. However you create it is the right way because it will reflect your style.

I just did a program, and I asked a participant, Julie, if I could use her list as an example. Here is Julie's list just as she wrote it, so not everything on it may make sense to you. It doesn't have to. The only person that it needs to make sense to is Julie, just as your list needs to make sense only to you. However, the longer the list, the more options you'll have to choose from.

Julie's List

Strengths	*Talents*	*Passions*
Compassionate	Graphic design	Animals/cats
Detail oriented	Landscaping	Tulips
Helpful	Jewelry design	Fashion
Kind	Musical	Piano
Smart	Research	Reading fiction
Healthy	Coordinated	Hiking, outdoors
Social butterfly	Get people together	Humane Society
Disciplined	Great friend	Travel, Ireland
Creative	Endurance	Love stories
Action oriented	Supportive others	Tom
Romantic	Romantic	Romantic

To map out your positive core, highlight what you believe are your top strengths, qualities, and passions. Remember that your positive core will tend to evolve along with you.

Serious Mountains Require Serious Planning

Once you've outlined your positive core, you can begin planning a route that will capitalize on it. It is the planning that allows you to be smart about taking this risk and allows you to reduce the challenges involved in tackling this mountain. If you think about this as it might relate to Mount Everest, it may become clearer. To climb Everest even with a well-prepared team is clearly risky. To go there alone without a plan, supplies, food, oxygen, clothing, climbing tools, and a map would be a fool's errand. It is your plan that allows you to minimize your risk.

In today's world of too much to do and too little time, most of us do not actually sit down and create a detailed plan of attack for our mountains. In some cases, it is unnecessary; just thinking through the plan can be enough. However, if you are tackling a mountain that could seriously jeopardize your life, finances, career, emotional health, or spiritual well-being, then it's critical to take the time and acquire the expertise to create a full-scale plan. If you don't, you won't be taking an intelligent risk.

To do this I suggest you pick up a project management book that deals with your specific goal and potentially find an expert in this area who can help you. If you're considering anything that could have a serious impact on your life but you don't plan, you are taking a dumb chance, not an intelligent risk.

IntelligentRisking Foundation

I'm a big believer in doing everything possible to synthesize the complex into something that is straightforward, easy to understand, and memorable. The IntelligentRisking foundation consists of just six key questions to remember:

- ✓ Who?
- ✓ What?
- ✓ When?
- ✓ Where?
- ✓ Why?
- ✓ How?

Using the IntelligentRisking foundation, you'll be able to look at quantitative information, found in traditional project management, as well as qualitative information, found in your own self-awareness. When you're able to blend these different factors and types of information, you can begin to craft a route that will work best for you.

As you seek quantitative or tangible information, you'll need to look at the issues that you can measure. You'll evaluate what you need versus what you have and identify how you intend to bridge the gap.

As you look for qualitative information, you'll want to consider the subjective side and the intangibles involved with your mountain. You need to explore your own perceived strengths, weaknesses, and preferences, taking into account any factors that are significant enough to affect your decisions. Even with positive risk, we need to take our weaknesses into consideration. Stay focused on your positive core, but be aware of your Achilles' heel.

The first step is to determine what you need. This requires information and doing your home-work to find out as much as possible about your mountain. In climbing, this is called "getting beta." This involves research that includes read-ing, studying, and spending time exploring your mountain. It also means talking to others who have climbed similar mountains and learning from their successes and failures.

As women, we need to remind ourselves that by definition, a risk is a risk. We'll never have every-thing we need. It will never be perfect. We will make mistakes and adjust appropriately. We should focus on our strengths and plan a route that will capi-talize on them. If you know you are not good at accounting, then hire someone who is; don't spend your own time and energy in that area.

Following is a list of specific questions tied to each of the six IntelligentRisking foundation pieces to help you started. As you read through the questions, those that most directly apply to you and your risk will probably pop out. The ones on this list may trigger other questions you need to ask. Write down your answers, other questions you think of, and notes to help you develop the best route.

Who?

✓ Who are the right people for my team?

✓ Who will I need to help me make my crux move?

✓ Who is on my team who shouldn't be?

✓ Who isn't on my team who should be?

✓ Who else is passionate about my mountain?

✓ Who believes in me and wishes me success?

✓ Who doesn't believe in me and secretly hopes I fail?

✓ Who am I trying to impress?

✓ Who can help me?

✓ Who could hurt or sabotage me?

✓ Who will benefit?

✓ Who else is involved?

✓ Who else has control over the outcome?

✓ Who is pressuring me?

✓ Who is holding me back?

✓ Who am I trying to please?

✓ Who is inspiring me?

✓ Who do I need to help as I go along?

What?

✓ What are the risks?

✓ What are the rewards?

✓ What are my invisible risks?

✓ What are my invisible rewards?

✓ What is my passion?

✓ What will I need to help me make my crux move?

✓ What is the worst that could happen?

✓ What is the best that could happen?

✓ What is the most realistic outcome?

✓ What can I afford to lose?

✓ What can I do to reduce the risks?

✓ What can I do to increase the rewards?

✓ What information do I need?

✓ What equipment, supplies, skills, training, talents, and other resources will I need?

✓ What equipment, supplies, skills, training, talents, and other resources do I have?

✓ What is the gap between what I need and what I have?

✓ What can I do to lessen the gap?

✓ What can I do to improve my chances for success?

✓ What makes this risk necessary?

✓ What needs to happen?

✓ What tasks are involved?

✓ What do I need to do?

✓ What do others need to do?

✓ What milestones do I need to achieve?

✓ What go/no-go decision points are necessary?

✓ What do I need to control?

✓ What do I need to let go of?

✓ What filters am I using?

✓ What are my strengths?

✓ What are my preferences?

✓ What are my weaknesses?

✓ What can I do to support others as I climb?

When?

✓ When will I start?

✓ When will I need to make my crux move?

✓ When will I have what I need?

✓ When do I want or need to reach my milestones?

✓ When do I want or need to accomplish my tasks, objectives, and goals?

✓ When do I need my equipment and supplies?

✓ When should I make my first move?

✓ When would be the best time to act?

✓ When would be the worst time to act?

✓ When will I need to reevaluate?

✓ When should I set my go/no-go points?

✓ When will I need to capitalize on my strengths?

✓ When should I be wary of my weaknesses?

✓ When will be my Olympic Moment of Opportunity?

✓ When will I celebrate along the way?

Where?

✓ Where will I find my crux move?

✓ Where will I find the expertise I'll need?

✓ Where will I find the people I need on my team?

✓ Where will I get the supplies I need?

✓ Where will I get the equipment I need?

✓ Where will I establish my base camp?

✓ Where will I get the training I need?

✓ Where will I get the resources I need?

✓ Where will I get the funding I need?

✓ Where will this take place?

✓ Where will I turn for help?

✓ Where will I keep everything?

✓ Where will I turn for support?

✓ Where will I get the information and research I need?

✓ Where will I need my go/no-go decision points?

Why?

✓ Why this mountain?

✓ Why this team?

✓ Why this risk?

✓ Why now?

✓ Why this route?

✓ Why am I passionate about this?

✓ Why am I afraid?

✓ Why am I waiting?

✓ Why not?

How?

✓ How will I make my crux move?

✓ How big is the gap between what I have and what I need?

✓ How will I close the gap and reduce my risk?

✓ How will I improve my chances for success?

✓ How will I find the team and other support I need?

✓ How will I get the equipment, supplies, skills, training, talents, and other resources I'll need?

✓ How will I manage my strengths and weaknesses and my preferences?

✓ How will I know when it's time to reevaluate?

✓ How will I challenge my filters?

✓ How will I get what I need?

✓ How will I train and otherwise prepare?

✓ How will I hold onto my passion?

✓ How will I tame my fears?

✓ How much stuff do I need?

✓ How much time will it all take?

✓ How much will this cost?

✓ How much can I afford?

✓ How will I help and support others as I
go along?

The Right Route

All of us know someone who is brilliant yet struggles to find success. I'm convinced that unless that person has chosen the wrong mountain, it comes down to climbing the wrong route.

Have you noticed how interviewing for a new job is a lot like a first date? Everyone is at his or her best, and extremely polite and optimistic. I'm convinced the best day on any job is the day before you start, because on that fateful first day of work, you begin to understand that things aren't quite as wonderful as you thought.

That's how it was for me when I started working for Coors. Since I was going to be responsible for new product development and sales, I wanted to find out on my first day exactly how many "new" products were truly ready to go. The response was, "None." And I thought, *Well, that makes it harder.* Then I asked, "What where you talking about during my interview?" That's when they started to explain.

As it turns out, Joe Coors had gone on an overnight business trip and had taken only one dress shirt with him. (That's what men tend to do: pack one shirt for one meeting. Women, in contrast, pack options for overnight business trips.) When he went to put on his one shirt, it had three broken buttons. He was thoroughly annoyed and decided right then that Coors would make an unbreakable men's dress shirt button. He had the passion, and the mountain was clear. Even the route was fairly obvious since Coors not only made beer but was also a huge manufacturer of technical ceramics.

Joe Coors decided that this button would make the perfect product to start up a company, Ceramicon, to launch ceramic products in the consumer arena. The company spent the next two years working on the development of an unbreakable button. It came up with a virtually indestructible button made out of transformation-toughened zirconium. This button was so tough it could practically stop a bullet.

Ceramicon was planning on success and had lined up Arrow, one of the largest dress shirt manufacturers in the world, to buy the button. It appeared to be a match made in heaven. But there was a catch: the button cost more for Coors to make than Arrow would ever dream of paying for it. The obvious solution was to find a way to lower the price, and Ceramicon tried everything imaginable. But no matter how much they reduced the cost, it was still too expensive. Finally they gave up on the button, determining that it just couldn't be sold.

When I joined the company, I was fresh, from an entirely different background, and obviously not burned out on the button. But when you sign on for a new business/new product/sales type job, the first thing you are given is your dollar goal, and it doesn't matter if you don't have a product to sell. I knew I needed to get creative. I asked them to tell me more about this button.

It's important to understand that the technical ceramic industry has an industrial mind-set of low margins and high volumes. It may sell a product for only a few pennies but then sells millions and millions of them so the math still works. My professional experience at Disney and Hallmark was quite different: I came from a premium pricing background where I learned how to position, market, and sell the intangibles.

With nothing to lose and a sales goal to make, I decided to go after the button. I knew we needed a different route to get up this mountain, so I drew on my expertise of marketing premium products. The button was given a name, The Diamond Z. We created its own logo. We hired a public relations firm to do a national PR campaign, including the *Today Show.* We doubled the price. It was now not just an unbreakable button; it was an environmentally friendly alternative to all pearl and shell buttons. Our first sales calls were not to mass marketers like Arrow but to top-name designers like Ralph Lauren. The first order came from the environmentally conscientious Nordstrom. That button, the one that "couldn't be sold," became one of the single most profitable products in the company.

Coors had the passion and knew the mountain but had chosen the wrong route and was then unable to adjust to the obstacles. Although this book is not specifically about diversity, this is a perfect example of why diversity is so valuable. When you create a team that blends diverse backgrounds, you gain additional perspectives, expertise, and abilities from which to better tackle difficult challenges.

Your Response to Critical Question #4: What's My Route?

It's now time for you to determine the best route for you to climb your mountain. As you think it through, remember that it's important that your route capitalizes on your strengths, talents, and positive core while protecting against your weaknesses. This is what will maximize your chances for success. A route that works beautifully for one person can spell disaster for the next. Your route should be uniquely yours and be based on IntelligentRisking foundation of who, what, when, where, how, and why.

Critical Question #5
What's My Contingency Plan?

Do not marry your plan.

Dynamic Route Finding

Some people love to plan. They love it so much that they spend an inordinate amount of time developing what they think will be a perfect plan. They become so vested in it that they have a tendency to fall in love with it. When they face an unanticipated situation that they had not planned for, they can become quite reluctant to give up on their plan. They become inflexible and resistant to change. It's essential that you avoid becoming so invested in your plan that you refuse to deviate from it. You can marry anyone you want (as long as you love the person); however, don't marry your plan.

No matter how much you study, how many people you interview, and how much time you've spent planning, once you're up on the rock, your perspective changes. Nothing is ever quite the way you thought it would be. Route finding is a fluid, dynamic process that changes based on numerous variables, including weather, team endurance, and supplies.

Dynamic route finding is like on-the-job training. What are the critical components of your plan? What components are absolutely essential for you to have a successful climb? Think about what you might do for a backup. If something is working, how can you do more of it? If you know who you want on the team and they aren't available, how will you adjust? If you can't get the training, what will you do? What if the money runs out too soon?

Planning for contingencies requires that you ask the "What if?" question for the key components of your plan. For example, a rope is an important piece of equipment. What if something happened to it? Do you have a spare? Do you have slings that you could use in its place? Did you pack a parachute?

You will need to focus on asking "What if?" from a positive perspective. This may at first be difficult for you; however, if you look at even negative scenarios from a positive perspective, you are much more likely to come up with creative contingencies that will work. If you insist on looking at negative situations with a negative perspective, you will most certainly wake the monster within.

The need to develop contingencies is a lesson I learned over and over again during my new product and business development days. For example, we needed to ask "What if?" in case a toy was a flop so that we would be prepared to minimize our losses over excess inventory. We also needed to ask "What if?" in case a toy was a huge hit, ironically for the same reason: to minimize our loss of potential sales. Toy cycles or life spans are short, so we needed to have contingency

plans in place to both immediately stop production and immediately expand production based
on the new product's success. If the toy took off
and we couldn't meet demand, we'd miss out on
a tremendous sales opportunity, which would
translate into lost dollars.

The key to dynamic route finding is to plan a
route that builds in flexibility. Just as with Coors,
you can be clear about your mountain and have a
tremendous amount of passion; however, if you
choose a route that doesn't work and then can't
adjust, you'll struggle to find success.

Perhaps it's because of my background that I
love backup plans. They have saved me so many
times that they are second nature to me now.
Even if I'm simply setting up a coffee date with
someone, I give that person my cell phone number or pick out an alternative place to meet, just
in case.

Once you start your climb, things will inevitably change, and you'll need to be adapt-
able. Too often when women hit a dead end, they
jump to the conclusion that they have chosen
the wrong mountain or that something is wrong
with them. Perhaps you are simply at your own
crux move.

> If you create a good plan, then maybe
> you need to let go a bit, trusting in
> your flexibility, resourcefulness,
> and ability to figure it all out.

Spontaneous versus Planned Risks

There are several different kinds of risk. We've been looking at the type of risk that is premeditated and thought through. But sometimes you find yourself in a spontaneous situation that requires you to take a risk and there's no time to plan, let alone have a contingency plan. All we can do is jump on the route and figure it out as we go along.

Sometimes You Just Have to Jump In

Barb Weiman was visiting a high school in an unofficial role, delivering brownies for her granddaughter's birthday. Although Barb has dedicated herself to children as an educational counselor for almost fifty years, she hadn't anticipated what was about to happen.

It was a tough high school with students from a number of different schools around the city. There were gang members from opposing gangs, and the fighting between them had escalated to a red alert status. If the teachers heard a gang call, they locked the classroom doors and called the police.

The school was set up in a Y floor plan. Barb had just gotten to the middle of the three intersecting halls when she heard a cry from the end of one of the hallways. She'd had enough experience to know the meaning of that sound. Then she heard a responding cry from an opposing gang at the end of the opposite hallway. Barb was caught in the middle. Although she has a reputation for not being intimidated by anyone or anything, she wasn't prepared for two rival gangs bearing down on her ready to fight.

Not knowing exactly what to do, she trusted her instincts and held her ground. Seeing a grandmother in the middle of the hall wasn't exactly what either gang had expected, so they were momentarily caught off guard. Knowing she wouldn't have the upper hand for long, Barb started passing out brownies and asking everyone to try them.

Barb is a fabulous cook, and she had these would-be combatants hooked after just one bite of her brownies and literally eating out of the palm of her hand. This was quite a shock to the police, who showed up minutes later anticipating a gang war. Barb turned around what could have been a disastrous situation with her quick wits, willingness to risk, and some incredible brownies.

Sometimes You Get Pushed In

I have always envied those who knew what they wanted to do when they grew up. I wasn't that lucky. The only thing I knew for sure growing up is that I wanted to do something that would make a difference. I wanted to help people. Starting your own business is a risk that I'd recommend people plan for; however, that wasn't how it happened for me.

When I had my first child, I decided that my mountain was to be a great mom, so I left the corporate arena and went the more traditional route by staying home full time. Three years later with three little boys in tow, I was having second doubts. I remember picking up nine bags of disposable diapers at the store and the young man ringing up my purchases asked me if I knew

I had three different sizes of diapers. I assured him that I was perfectly aware, as all three boys were in diapers at the same time. At that moment, something clicked, and I knew the traditional route wasn't right for me.

I decided that perhaps a consulting opportunity where I could work part time might be the answer. The first two organizations I contacted both offered me full-time jobs. It was not what I was looking for, but I decided to try giving the working full-time route a go. Many of my friends were climbing their mountains successfully with this route, so why not me? I accepted a full-time position with Coors and hired a nanny to look after the boys.

It took almost three years to decide that this route wasn't right for me either. That's when I realized I wasn't clear on how I defined success, and I needed to think it through. I was still working full time but had started toying around with some other options. I wondered if cutting back on the travel and perhaps working only four days a week in the office might make a good compromise. I decided to test the water and throw that option out to my boss. The following day, we talked over lunch, and by the end of that day, to my complete surprise, I was no longer an employee of Coors.

Instead, I was a consultant, and Coors was my first customer.

I honestly didn't know what hit me. It certainly isn't how I'd recommend anyone start a company. However, since it was the right mountain, it all worked out, and it turned out to be the right route for me. As I think back, I'm afraid that if I had known at the time how hard this would be, I never would have tried it. In the first year, I lost forty thousand dollars, all the money I had. (You may wonder why I lost that much. If I'd had sixty thousand dollars, I'd have lost that too.) At some point when your back is against the wall but you want it badly enough, you'll find a way to make it work.

When you travel a lot, you tend to see a lot of movies on airplanes. A few summers ago I saw bits and pieces of *Maid in Manhattan* seven times on my various trips. The one line I loved in that movie came as the maid was fired and she found out the butler was also leaving because he had been fired for trying to help her. When she tried to apologize to him, he turned to her and said something like, "Life has a funny way of opening doors that you should have found for yourself." The key is to recognize them and walk through while they are still open. This means that decisions involving risk can come flying at you before you've had your first cup of coffee, or they may come as the result of careful thought and planning. Life is a wonderful mix of the spontaneous and the planned. The key is to live life to the fullest, trust in yourself, and use IntelligentRisking to help you with the pivotal decisions you'll face.

No Perfect Plan

Whether the risk is planned or spontaneous, we are not looking for a perfect plan. Rather, we are looking for a great plan. The truth is that some of us love the planning part more than the doing part. We'd like nothing better than to spend all of our time acquiring information. It can become an easy excuse not to start.

Needing a solid plan with every possibility thought out makes a strong argument. Yet it's easy to get so caught up in creating the perfect plan that you'll completely miss your window of opportunity. Since there is no perfect plan, set yourself a deadline, and do the best you can in the time you have.

Your Response to Critical Question #5: What's My Contingency Plan?

Now it's time to think through your plan with a positive perspective and create a backup for any critical components. Develop contingencies for anything that might keep you from reaching your goal.

9

Strategy III: Build Your Courage

Roar Like a Lion

Now that you have chosen your mountain and planned your route, it is time to build your passion so that you can push through your fears. It's time to learn how to roar like a lion—even if you're feeling like a kitten.

Critical Question #6
How Do I Visualize Success?

Trust that you will live up to
the image you have of yourself.

Imagine the Future

Successful risk takers are constantly visualizing their successes, past, present, and future. Visualization is a critical component of IntelligentRisking. How do medical students make it through their internship? They visualize themselves as successfully practicing doctors saving people's lives. How do prisoners of war survive? They visualize themselves as free. These mental pictures create powerful, compelling futures, so it's important to make your visualizations meaningful.

In one of my programs, one woman's mountain was to lose fifty pounds. Her visualization was getting on the scale and weighing fifty pounds less. That was not good enough! I don't think that image would stave off the doughnut urge in the middle of the night. I asked her to reconsider, and the new picture she created was much more compelling: she was wearing skin-tight white jeans (a risk for any woman), strappy sandals, and a midriff-baring top, and her hair was blowing in the breeze from the surf as she walked past her old boyfriend. In the background, the song "I'm Too Sexy for My Shirt" was playing. Now that's a clear visualization! I told her that I thought there may be more than one mountain going on, but if it worked for her, then it worked for me. You may find it interesting to know that I met her again one year later at the same conference, and that visualization had worked for her: she had lost that fifty pounds and was a new woman. More striking than her slim figure was her radiant smile and confident attitude.

The Placebo Effect

Courage means confidence. In the early 1900s, doctors gave their patients pills to help them sleep, ease depression, and provide a pick-me-up. Often those little pills they handed out in reds and greens were simply sugar pills, or placebos. The reason they worked remarkably well was that the patients believed they were getting an actual drug, and they expected it to work.

Alan Alda hosted a fascinating show that premiered February 18, 2003, on PBS. Titled "Scientific American Frontiers Program #1307 'The Wonder Pill,'" it explored the placebo effect and its power on the human mind. Andy Leuchter, a physician, had conducted a study that was able to measure and quantify the placebo effect. The bottom line is that placebos have no physical effect on the body, but they do have a physiological effect that can trigger the brain, which in turn has a physiological effect that can make a disease change its course.

Leuchter's study measured the effect placebos have on brain activity through electroencephalograms. As Alda said during the show, "While it may all be in the mind, the placebo effect is real and measurable." Never did he or anyone else say that placebos work for all people. In a number of cases, they had no effect; in others, the positive shift was temporary. In most cases, once the patient realized it was a placebo, he or she relapsed. However, the placebos in this study did create positive results in 40 percent of the patients. These results encourage researchers to look at a new world of possibilities in health care.[1]

Visions That Dance in Your Head

It's clear that our minds are one of the greatest unexplored frontiers, and our thoughts have significant influence over what happens. That's why it is so important for you to focus on your accomplishments, give yourself credit, and visualize yourself as successful. Even if you aren't as successful at this moment as you wish, the surest way to get there is to visualize yourself as successful. That single action, the power of a vision, is the trick that enables us to open up and tap into things inside ourselves that we don't yet understand.

Your own vision of your success must be as dramatic and compelling as your mountain is difficult. The greater the obstacles are, the more often you'll need to draw on your visualization to help you meet the challenge. That means you need to make your vision clear, fun, and worth the effort.

When you reach your summit, will you celebrate? If so, will it be a huge party or an intimate affair? Will it be at sunrise, sunset, or another time? Where will your party be: at a castle, a beach, or a spa? Who will be there? Will you invite the press, or will you need to hide from the media? What band is playing? Or is it an orchestra? What food will you serve? Will there be water with lemon, diet soft drinks, or champagne flowing? Visualizing success will allow you to push through your fears and fuel your passion.

Your Response to Critical Question #6: How Do I Visualize Success?

Now it's time for you to create a compelling future for yourself by developing a vivid and compelling visualization that is so powerful that you'll be irresistibly drawn toward it.

Critical Question #7
What Are My Passions?

Failure is impossible.
—*Susan B. Anthony*

Identifying Your Rewards

You have chosen your mountain, defined success, and visualized yourself at the top; now it's time to focus on what rewards are involved. What are the benefits you see? What will you gain? What is the best that can happen? Rewards are subjective, so take the time to write out all the rewards that you think are possible.

Identifying Your Passions

What passions do these rewards tap into for you? What is it about these rewards that fire you up? Take the time to consider all your passions that relate to this mountain, and draw up a list. It is this list that will help you push through your fears.

Increasing Your Passion

There are many ways to increase your passion, and we'll look at several. In addition to visualizing yourself successfully reaching your goal, try surrounding yourself with people who believe in you and support your mountain.

Surrounding yourself with support is a tried-and-true formula and a powerful tactic. If you have support from family, friends, and coworkers, you are well on your way to success. If you interact on a consistent basis with others who share your passion, your path will be easier. If you find yourself surrounded by doomsayers who constantly remind you of your weaknesses, you are facing an uphill fight.

This is where being proactive is critical. Knowing that those who are negative are going to hold you back, you need to make a choice about whether you will accept, change, or reject this group. It's up to you.

Women Supporting Women

When it comes to risking successfully and building courage, a key for women is to support each other, support each other, and support each other. An excellent example of this comes from one of my clients, Jackson Walker, one of the oldest, largest, and most respected law firms in Texas. One might think that a law firm founded in 1887 might be less than progressive in the area of women's issues. Nothing could be further from the truth. Not only does the firm actively recruit and hire top female attorneys, it offers significant support to a number of women's groups within the community that are focused on helping women reach their full potential.

Jackson Walker doesn't just talk the talk. The value it has for female partners and its top female clients is expressed in a weekend retreat it sponsors for these women at a spa. The entire weekend is crafted to create an atmosphere of women supporting, nurturing, and building personal and professional relationships. The first evening at dinner, there were conversations between clients discussing how they could potentially use each other's services. New opportunities opened up for everyone attending. Men understand the value of these client appreciation weekends, and I'm glad to see that the male partners at Jackson Walker are supporting their partners in building networks of women supporting women.

In my programs, I ask how we women can better support each other. The following are ideas that have been proven to work.

Ideas for Supporting Each Other

✓ Encourage each other to take risks that matter.

✓ Start official or unofficial mentoring programs just for women. Each person has a mentor and is a mentor so that everyone is getting and giving.

✓ Find ways to promote each other and each other's ideas. If all things are equal, recommend a woman for the job.

✓ Promote each other's potential to each other and to men.

✓ In meetings, ask each other about our successes. I already have noted that we are regularly advised to blow our own horn more often, yet we tend not to. This provides us the opportunity to talk about our success in a way that feels comfortable to us and others.

✓ Cut out the water-cooler chatter. Unfortunate as it is, we can all get caught in some negative conversations about others that are unnecessary. As soon as it starts, you need to say, "Let's keep it positive." That works like a charm; everyone knows they should remain positive, and they'll respect the gentle reminder. (Note that this plan doesn't work so well an hour into the conversation.)

✓ Find a safe place to vent. For example, find a partner who will listen to your frustration and anger. This will provide both of you a safe place to get rid of the negative energy and leave with more productive thoughts.

✓ Continue to point out each other's strengths. It will remind you of your own.

✓ Focus on successes.

✓ Accept compliments with a smile and a thank-you.

✓ Help each other find the value in a mistake. For example, what's the lesson in it all, and what wisdom have you gained as a result?

✓ Practice taking everything less seriously. Try to stay calm, and build in more fun.

✓ When you ask questions in meetings, provide a context. For example, frame the questions in this way: "I understand, but I'd like you to clarify . . ."

✓ Give each other the benefit of the doubt.

✓ Acknowledge and thank the women who support you. If a woman recommends my program to another client who books me, for example, I send the person a gift certificate to a spa. I feel strongly that we need to thank all those who help us.

Change Agent

Equity Office Properties (EOP) is the largest publicly held office building owner and manager in the United States. This progressive company recognized that simply hiring talented women was not enough. The key was to create an environment in which these women would want to stay and develop their careers. In 2002, senior management group at Equity made the strategic decision to get more active behind their women's initiative program entitled Women In Management

Network (WIMN). I was fortunate enough to have my program, "Awaken the Leader Within—Intelligent-Risking for Women," chosen to help launch this new women's initiative across the country. I have now traveled to every regional Equity Office location presenting my program, and I have found working with this group of talented women an honor and a privilege.

Barb Kildow, director of investor communications for Equity, was responsible for organizing the event for the corporate group in Chicago. Barb, having more organization in her little finger than I will possess in a lifetime, encouraged all women in the Chicago group to attend. In addition to many others, Diane Morefield, senior vice president of investor relations for Equity Office and also the leader of Equity's WIMN, attended.

My presentations always involve a number of interactions between participants. During one interaction, Barb partnered with a senior woman in the information technology department. Barb's partner, the mother of four young children, was trying to build up her courage to speak with her (male) manager about the possibility of a four-day workweek. She was afraid to broach the subject for fear not only that her request would be turned down but also that by even bringing up the subject, she'd be written off as not serious enough about her career.

She didn't realize that Barb works closely with Diane Morefield, who was herself hired years earlier on a four-day workweek by Richard Kincaid, then chief financial officer and now president and chief executive officer of Equity Office. Diane's flexible schedule has worked out brilliantly for her and the company. However, as in all other organizations, not everyone is completely convinced that some of these progressive ideas work. Barb urged her partner to call Diane to set up lunch and get some advice. Of course, Barb also mentioned this to Diane, who was more than happy to help.

Diane found herself facing a challenge. It wasn't the lunch; it was the meeting she would be having the following day. She was scheduled to give an update to all senior management of Equity Office on the status and successes of the women's initiative. It was a unique opportunity because this meeting was going to include an additional two levels of management.

It was clear from the unnamed partner's experience in information technology that there were still women in the organization afraid even to broach the subject of flexible work schedules.

Diane felt that if she could clearly explain the importance of the women's initiative during her update, that change would filter down. This meeting was Diane's chance to make a difference.

An accomplished, polished professional, Diane knew intuitively that she was going to have to do something different to get this group's attention. She wanted the company's senior management team to truly understand that flexible work schedules are critically important if they wanted to keep talented women at Equity Office. To make an impact, she decided to add a picture at the end of her presentation of her three children. Any woman knows that it is a risk to blur the line between professional and personal. It was a risk few men would understand, let alone ever take.

Until the end of her presentation, she wasn't sure if she would show that last slide, knowing she could conclude without hitting the button one last time. As she told this story, she had me hanging on the edge of my seat. Did she push the button? Yes. Up on the screen in front of all the executives at Equity Office was a picture of her children. She told them that only because of the flexibility of a four-day workweek was she able to balance her professional and personal life, a challenge both men and women face.

I asked her why she took the risk. As Diane reflected back on the IntelligentRisking program she had attended the day before, she realized that if she wanted other women to take risks, she needed to set the example. She had to stand up for what she believed in. Diane also felt that if she could prove, on a personal level, to the management team that a flexible schedule does work, then maybe other women in the organization would be given the opportunity as well.

I asked her about the response she received. She said that several of the people in the meeting came up and congratulated her on her presentation. There is no doubt that not everyone liked her blurring that carefully guarded boundary between work and home; however, everyone walked away respecting her courage to take that risk.

Women supporting women is a powerful change agent. I'd like you to commit to one action you'll take to support other women better and write it down. It may be something you'll start doing, or it may be something you'll stop doing. It may represent a huge risk, or no risk. However, if each of us could commit to just one action to help each other more, then we are all ahead of the game.

One interesting postscript: Barb's partner never called Diane. Granted, she didn't know that Barb had spoken to Diane, so she may have thought Diane would be too busy to see her. I don't know why she didn't call, but by not taking that risk, she missed an important opportunity.

Your Response to Critical Question #7: What Are My Passions?

Determine what genuine passions you have around this mountain and your rewards. Think through what it is that you care about and why it matters so much to you. No matter how great your passion is, develop a plan that will help you increase it.

Critical Question #8
What Are My Fears?

If you run from your fears,
they will chase you.

Identifying Your Risks

The risks involved on this mountain are probably obvious to you. The question to ask is, "Are they real? What are the odds they'll happen? What can I do to minimize them?" To take this risk in the smartest way possible, revisit your plan to see if there is anything else you can do to reduce your risk.

It's also important to remember that risk is a matter of perspective. If it keeps you up at night ask yourself if the risk is real. Two friends, both leaving their jobs, may have the same mountain and yet see the risks quite differently. One woman may feel that losing touch with those she has worked so closely with is a risk, while the other woman may see getting away as a reward, a fresh start. Take a moment to think through the risks as you see them and how you can minimize their impact.

Identifying Your Fears

Given the risks associated with your mountain, what are your fears? Identifying your fears requires that you look behind the risks to see what it is you're afraid of. It requires that you look a little deeper still to understand what in your past or in your personal makeup contributes to these fears. What are your Ghosts of Risks Past? What is it about these fears that might hold you back? What fears do you need to face?

Facing Your Fears

Facing your fears is different from identifying and understanding them. It is also much more difficult. I've been paragliding for six years. Last year I had a rough landing and broke my tailbone. It was clearly pilot error. Knowing that the accident was my own fault did not help my confidence. I still wanted to fly, but I found myself making all kinds of excuses to ensure I didn't have time to fly. Basically my passion hadn't diminished, but my fears had grown and were beginning to overpower it.

Finally, I ran out of good excuses and decided I'd get back in the saddle (or harness) again. I knew I was a little nervous, but I didn't realize how scared I was until we were driving up to launch, and I started crying. No one was more surprised than I. I had no idea I had so much fear that I hadn't dealt with.

My greatest fear was that I was inadequate and didn't have the skill, knowledge, or competence to fly. That is a scary thought, and it should be. The last thing anyone wants is a pilot in the air who isn't qualified. Yet I know that I have excellent ground-handling, launching, and landing skills. Landing is the critical piece to this puzzle because that's where pilots get hurt. I realized that day that understanding and talking about fears is not the same as facing them.

Once I faced my fears and got past the tears, I still wasn't ready to fly. I could have, but I wasn't prepared emotionally. However, I was ready for some incremental risk taking. That means to take the first step, so I got my paragliding wing out, laid it out, and began to practice my ground-handling skills. Once those skills were solid, I decided to start hiking up the hill.

At the top, I was the only woman (which isn't unusual). I spent the day practicing bringing up my wing to launch and watching the other pilots. The practice reduced my fear, while watching the other pilots fly fueled my passion. I had made the shift: my passion was now greater than my fear, and I was ready to launch. They say you only have one "first" flight and that no other flight will ever compare, but that flight certainly came close.

Take some time to think through and understand what fears you may need to face. I realize that this is a difficult challenge, yet it is these fears that may stop you from reaching your goal. At a minimum, you need to be aware of what fears may lure you into quitting too soon. Writing them down next to your risks may help you deal with them.

Reducing Your Fears

Fear is a double-edged sword: it keeps you safe but can stop you from doing many things. Risk by definition is always risky, so there will always be some fear. The key is not to eliminate your fears but to feel the fear without letting it control you; you need to understand your fears and manage them so that the choices you make are your own. There are many ways to reduce your fears. One is to identify, understand, and face them. Another is preparation.

Being prepared is following through on the plan you developed to acquire the training, resources, equipment, and supplies you need. The more prepared you are, the more comfortable you'll feel. The hazard is that it's easy to stall out in an effort to become as prepared as you possibly can. You will never be completely prepared. Don't let yourself fall into the Waiting Place. There will always be more you can do, so set yourself some goals with deadlines, do your best, and then move forward.

Your Response to Critical Question #8: What Are My Fears?

Now it's time for you to ask yourself what is the worst that can happen if you climb this mountain. Take the time to note down all the significant risks that come to mind. Now list the fears that rest behind those risks, and create a plan to help you reduce those fears.

Critical Question #9
What Are My Invisible Risks and Rewards?

Regrets don't come from taking risks that failed. Regrets come from failing to take risks.

The Risk of Regret

If you decide you don't believe you have the courage that it's going to take to climb your mountain, ask yourself before you turn back, "What will it be like if I don't climb? How will I feel about myself if I quit? Will I have regrets?"

There is an inherent and significant risk in paragliding. As I faced my fear about trying to fly again, it would have been easy for me to say, "I'm not going to fly again because it's too dangerous." However, for me, there was another risk, an invisible risk: the risk of regret, of quitting a sport I love without giving myself one more chance. My decision was to continue to fly; if one day I choose to stop, then I, not my fear, will be making the decision.

If it truly isn't your mountain and you decide to turn away, you may feel that an enormous weight has been lifted from your shoulders. If it really is your mountain and you turn away, you may have the gnawing feeling of regret and disappointment.

The Reward of Believing in Yourself

Now consider what invisible rewards may exist for you. One of the reasons I decided to try paragliding one more time is that I was clear on my invisible reward: I knew that no matter how my flight went, I would be proud of myself for giving it this try. By understanding your own invisible rewards, you may find an increase in your passion around your goal.

Some people fear failing so much that they don't try, which takes away confidence and adds to their fear. Ask yourself:

✓ Even if this risk turns on me, how will I feel about myself for trying?

✓ If things don't go exactly as planned, will I be smarter and wiser for the experience?

✓ Even if it all blows up, will I be proud to tell others I went for it?

✓ What do I see as my invisible rewards?

Your Response to Critical Question #9: What Are My Invisible Risks and Rewards?

Now it's time for you to ask yourself two questions: "What if I don't climb this mountain? How will I feel?" and "What if I climb, and it doesn't turn out the way I hope? How will I feel?" These two questions will allow you to identify your invisible risks and rewards.

Critical Question #10
What's My Courage Ratio?

You gain strength, courage and
confidence by every experience in which
you really stop to look fear in the face.
You must do the thing that you
think you cannot do.

—*Eleanor Roosevelt*

Building Your Courage

Passion greater than fear equals courage. Do you
have the courage you need to tackle your mountain? If not, then you need to find ways to build
your passion and reduce your fear. Although our
mountains may be quite different, we all share
the same basic fears.

I'll take a chance and share with you my personal struggle over writing this book. The risk I
saw was that I might not be able to articulate my
thoughts clearly and in a way that would help
other women. I was afraid that I might say the
wrong thing or say too much or too little. I took
my responsibility to write a great book so seriously that I wanted the book to be perfect. That
risk tapped into my fear that I wouldn't be good
enough. The reason I share such personal feel-

ings is to ensure that you understand that everyone has fears. The key is to face them and then do what you need to do, understanding that nothing is perfect.

The reward I saw in writing this book was the possibility of helping other women see within themselves their talent, wisdom, and potential. The other reward I saw was sending a strong message to my sons about not giving up when it gets hard. I had told them five years ago that I was going to write this book. Last year when Joey asked me what had happened to my book, I didn't have a good answer. I knew that although I might be willing to let myself down, I was not willing to let my sons see me give up on a dream. I did not want to be a quitter in their eyes. Both the invisible risk and reward tapped into my passion to make a difference. Although my fears had held me back, my passion finally won out. You are holding the proof in your hands.

The Ebb and Flow of Courage

Courage is an intangible that ebbs and flows as you climb. There will be days when you climb exceptionally well, and you'll feel the courage of a lioness. Then there will be days that you climb very tenuously and feel as fragile as a lion cub.

The key is to anticipate these fluxes so that on a difficult day, you don't jump to the wrong conclusion and believe that you don't have what it takes to climb this mountain or that you're on the wrong route.

There is a saying that "all storms pass," and they do. If you feel that you are in the middle of a dark storm, try to sit it out. Give the situation some time. Reflect on what and why things are happening, and give yourself some time to think before you make a hasty decision to give up.

Your Response to Critical Question #10: What's My Courage Ratio?

Now it's time for you to calculate your courage ratio as it pertains to climbing the mountain you've identified. If your passion is greater than your fear, you'll have the courage to act. If it is not, it will be time to build your courage and reduce your fear. If you still do not have the courage, then it is time to reevaluate your mountain. Ask yourself:

✓ Is it the right mountain?
✓ Whose mountain is it?

✓ Am I on the right route?

✓ Have I looked at my possibilities?

✓ Am I being flexible and resourceful?

If you still feel strongly that this is a goal you want to pursue, you will need to develop a plan to build your courage and trust in yourself.

Critical Question #11
What's My Courage Touchstone?

It is not how much we do, but how much love we put in the doing.

It is not how much we give, but how much love we put in the giving."
—*Mother Teresa of Calcutta*

Reconnecting with Your Own Courage

I have the unusual perspective that coming up with courage is fairly easy. Think about it. You want to try something new. It feels exciting. You tell some friends. They get excited for you. The momentum builds. What I believe is extraordinarily difficult is holding on to your courage six months or a year later when times get tough. When you're alone and wondering, "Am I doing the right thing?" that's when it gets hard.

This struggle with courage is something that we can anticipate because it happens to even the bravest people. Although we are the only one who can give ourselves courage, sometimes we need to reconnect with our own courage. We can prepare by having a courage touchstone: a person, a place, a time, or a memory to help us reconnect with our original fortitude. When I begin to doubt myself, I think of one of my courage touchstones. If I think of my best friend, Valari, I see the look of confidence in her eyes as I hear her voice telling me how talented I am, and then I start to feel how much she believes in me. That allows me to look at myself from her perspective, which reconnects me to my own courage. Your courage touchstone is anything that helps you do this.

Finding Your Courage Touchstone

Each of us has many different courage touchstones, and we find them in some unusual ways. For myself, I go back a few summers. I was meeting my friend Brian; when he arrived, he was on his way to grant a rush wish for the Make-A-Wish Foundation. Being a wish grantor is a lot like being a fairy godmother. As a trained volunteer, you meet and interview children who have life-threatening illnesses about the one thing they wish for. The Make-A-Wish Foundation determines if their wish is feasible and pulls all the details together. Then as a wish grantor, you get to deliver the wish to the child.

Brian had been a wish grantor for many years and invited me to go with him. The wish was to a Russian boy who, with his mother, was brought to Denver to receive treatment for his leukemia. His nickname was Sasha.

Since neither Sasha nor his mother spoke any English, an interpreter was at the apartment. Make-A-Wish, like all other organizations, requires a great deal of paperwork. Brian, the interpreter, and Sasha's mother sat at the kitchen table filling out forms, which left me alone with Sasha.

Sasha was seven years old, and at the time, my sons were six, eight, and nine, so you know he had a special place in my heart. When I left that day I realized two truths: one, I had fallen hopelessly in love with Sasha, and two, no matter the circumstances, no matter where they're from, when it's time to go, little boys can't find their shoes.

Sasha's wish to visit Disney World was granted. However, just coming to America was like Disney World to him, so this trip was the frosting on his cake. I hope that everyone has the opportunity to see a wish like this come true. The transformation in Sasha was dramatic. He came back from Disney World with so much life and vitality that it was like meeting a new child.

Now I was faced with a difficult choice. I knew Sasha didn't know anyone or have any friends in Denver. Should I invite him over and include him in my life? That would be a risk. I was already in love with him, so what if something did happen? It would break my heart and also probably affect my own boys.

But then I thought about how much we had to offer him, including all the toys a seven-year-old boy could want. I decided to call a family meeting. I explained to my sons that Sasha had a life-threatening illness and asked if they thought we should invite him over to play. They looked at me as if I'd grown another head. A boy to come over and play—*of course,* we should invite him over. Then they asked, "Why are we having a family meeting about something like this?" Before he came over the first time, they had their heads shaved so he wouldn't feel out of place.

I was concerned about having Sasha over to our house since my boys are not quiet by any stretch of the imagination. I told them that Sasha didn't have the strength they had and asked them to tone it down a bit. I started them all out playing cards, which quickly bored them all to tears. That's when my son Nick looked over at Sasha and said, as only an eight-year-old boy could, "You don't look like you are dying to me. Let's go play." And they all took off.

My sons were willing to give Sasha the gift that I wasn't: they treated him like a regular kid (and they all ended up terrorizing the entire neighborhood, as my boys are wont to do). Over the summer, we all fell in love with Sasha. I spent the summer pursuing various legal possibilities to keep Sasha here with us after he got better, but in August, the doctors determined the treatment was no longer effective. Sasha and his mother would have to return to Russia.

On the morning he left, as I was seeing him off, he looked pleadingly into my eyes and said, "Please don't make me go. I want to stay here with you." I had to say good-by. In October, Sasha died. Did he break my heart? Yes. Was it worth the risk? Yes.

Some of the greatest lessons I have learned in my life I learned from that little seven-year-old Russian boy who didn't speak much English. He taught me to take the risk of living life. Few of the risks we take will turn out just the way we plan. Yet if you take the right risk for the right reason, it always turns out right.

Sasha taught me that as important as the outcome is, just as important is who you become for having taken the risk. Because of Sasha, I'm now on the bone marrow donor transplant list, as well as a wish grantor for Make-A-Wish Foundation—neither of which I would have had the courage to do without Sasha. I have a wish board up in my office with pictures of all of the children that I have granted wishes to. Every time life gets tough, I walk over to it, and my problems fall back into perspective.

Whenever I lose sight of my courage—and I do just like everyone else—I think of Sasha. He will always be one of my courage touchstones, and I will always hear his voice say, *I believe in you. You can do this.*

Take a moment, and think of where you will turn when your own fears overwhelm you. What person, place, time, or memory will help you reconnect with your own courage?

Your Response to Critical Question #11: What's My Courage Touchstone?

Now it's time for you to choose your own courage touchstone. Decide on at least one person, place, poem, memory, or something else that will help you reconnect with your courage when you begin to doubt yourself.

10

Strategy IV: Climb Strong!

The Most Critical Step Is the First One

Now that you have chosen your mountain, planned your route, and built your courage, it's time to take the most important next step: climb strong!

Critical Question #12
What Do I Need to Let Go?

> How many cares one loses when one decides not to be something but to be someone.
>
> —*Coco Chanel*

Letting Go

At the beginning of this book, I described the crux move, the most difficult part of any climb. It's the move you must make, or you go no farther. It is similar to the risks you need to take to reach your goal. The big difference is that on a climb, the crux moves are often marked, along with suggestions on how to climb them. In life, that rarely happens. These moves tend to be surprises that are difficult to anticipate. The best advice on how to make your own crux moves is to understand that you will face them. You will be tested, perhaps to the edge of some preconceived limits, and you'll get through it.

I'm in the middle of doing research on how much of our talents, skills, and abilities we are currently using. Initial results indicate that less than 10 percent of us are using 90 percent of our talents, skills, and abilities; 20 percent are using 80 percent; and about 60 percent of us are using only 60 percent. Clearly we have more potential to make those crux moves than we may realize.

The monster within is often made up of a combination of fear, anger, and ego. It is one of the most dangerous and insidious of the invisible risks. Even when you start out with self-assurance, the monster within can sneak up on you. Obstacles that shake your confidence allow self-doubt to creep into your thinking and rumble around in your psyche, jeopardizing your mission. As Laura Day says in her book, *The Circle,* "Dread undermines our commitment to creation. We find ourselves swallowed by anger, envy and grief over what is not, instead of committed to create what can be."[1]

The Cowardly Lion, the Tin Man, and the Scarecrow in *The Wizard of Oz* all suffered because they doubted themselves. They went searching elsewhere for what they had inside themselves all along. Although you may not be able to anticipate what your crux move might be, if you understand that you will face one, then you won't be quite so quick to listen to the whispers of the monster.

Your Response to Critical Question #12: What Do I Need to Let Go?

Now it's your turn to decide what to let go so that you can move forward. In climbing, just as in the rest of life, you must let go to make your next move.

Critical Question #13
How Will I Embrace My Adventure?

Mistakes are merely outcomes that don't currently fit our expectations.

Seize the Day

Who knows what adventures your mountain will bring? There's no point in climbing anything if you aren't having fun. Since life doesn't seem to go out of its way to make anything easy for us, it's up to us to seize the day. As a wish grantor for the Make-A-Wish Foundation, I consider all my wish children to be special; however, as we talk about embracing your adventure, I'm especially reminded of Katherine.

When I go to interview a child about their wish, I love to make things special for them. I often do wishes with a partner, Brian O'Malley. The day we went to deliver Katherine's wish trip to Disney World, I had picked up a tiara and a magic wand for her. Sometimes Make-A-Wish sends small gifts along, like stationery, stickers, or books. We were very surprised when the gift she opened was a complete set of little girls' makeup, all in a shade of bright blue.

Katherine, with her tiara and wand, looked like quite a princess. She had a disease that was causing her spine to deteriorate and creating additional complications. She used a wheelchair and had limited dexterity with her hands, so she asked me to help out with the "makeover." I'm certainly not an experienced cosmetologist, so we quickly had blue sparkle powder and eye shadow all over both of us. Then I started on her nails with blue nail polish.

Once I finished, she looked down at her manicure. She frowned and not being able to remember my name said, "Princess Servant, you missed a spot." I fixed it, and she wheeled herself up to the full-length mirror in the hallway to survey the results of her makeover. That's when I heard her say, "Look out, Cinderella. There's a new princess coming to town!" Katherine is a great role model for finding the fun hidden in the challenges life hands us.

Fall Forward

Will you make mistakes? Of course you will. The key is to learn how to make mistakes that take you closer to, not further from, your goal. I'm convinced that one reason that I've found the success that I have is that I am very good at making mistakes. Practice makes perfect, and I've certainly had my share of practice. Over time, with a lot of mistakes to learn from, you begin to figure out which ones to make. Don't be afraid of them; just learn to make really smart ones so you can figure out the best path. Many times it's easier and quicker to try something, learn, and recover than it is to try to analyze the correct thing to do. I look at life like this: I'm five feet, six inches tall, and if I make a mistake and fall forward, then I'm almost six feet closer to my goal.

Your Response to Critical Question #13: How Will I Embrace My Adventure?

Now it's time for you to make a conscious decision to embrace your adventure and recognize that climbing is a dynamic and fluid process. That means things will change, and you need to stay flexible and resourceful. It's your choice to keep a bright heart and make the climb fun.

Critical Question #14
How Will I Climb Strong?

If you really want something and
really work hard and take advantage
of opportunities and never give up,
you will find a way.
—*Jane Goodall*

Even the first step on a climb creates a certain
amount of momentum that propels you upward
toward your goal.

The Butterfly Effect

In 1960, Edward Lorenz was a meteorologist at
MIT responsible for predicting weather patterns.
Computers had recently been introduced, and in
an effort to expedite the process, he decided to
round off a number in one of his calculations by
one-thousandth. He assumed that there would be
no significant variation in his predictions.

That small change—the equivalent of the puff
of wind created by one butterfly's wing—signifi-
cantly altered the projection creating a tropical
storm. Since then, the concept of a single action
generating the momentum to create a significant
change has been called the *butterfly effect.*

If you have ever mentioned an interest just once to family and friends—let's say you like clowns, as my mother once did—then you have seen the power of this effect. For years and years thereafter, Mom received miniature clowns in the form of ceramics, jewelry, papier-mâché, appliqués, and all manner of other forms from everyone. She got them on calendars, mugs, cards, clothing, and pictures, as well as an assortment of small clowns and larger ones to fill shelf after shelf. You will not believe how many clown products are available. Some are exquisitely beautiful, and some are simply ugly; my mother has them all over her house.

Even when she began telling people that she no longer liked clowns and had no more room for them, they still continue to arrive. (I've come to the conclusion that the attack of the clowns will never end.) Her love of clowns is slowly transforming itself into an intense dislike for them. She swears they multiply in the dark as she continues to find them and put them into her garage sales.

How big your first step is toward climbing your mountain is not as important as taking that first step. The momentum you create by declaring your mountain to others, checking out that one book, or making that first call is significant. That one action does indeed create a ripple effect that will help pull and push you toward your goal.

If we look at this concept in the bigger picture, consider that the one risk you take today, the one mountain you climb, will create new and significant opportunities for you in the future.

One Step at a Time

The key to starting is that first step. Think of one action that you are willing to take within the next week. Decide the best climbing partner for you, and commit to that person the one action you are going to take in the next seven days. This partnership will help put some positive pressure on you to make it happen. While doing a program for Equity Office Properties, I asked a woman what one step she would take. Her answer was profound: "It isn't a question of what I will do. It's a matter of what I'll stop doing."

It doesn't matter what your one action is, and it doesn't matter how big a step it is. What matters is that you take action to start building your momentum.

Climbing Procedure

In rock climbing, when you tie the rope from you to your partner, you're saying, "I trust you with my life." There is a level of seriousness that goes along with making that kind of commitment to another person.

There is an unwritten procedure that follows. Once each person ties her end of the rope into her own harness, she double-checks her own and her partner's knot for safety. Whoever is going to climb first is the climber, and whoever is holding the rope to keep the climber safe is the person belaying.

When the climber is ready, she says, "On belay." When the belayer is ready, she responds with, "Belay on." Then when the climber is actually going to start climbing, she says, "Climbing." Then the belayer says, "Climb on." This is the code. It's not a lot of words. You probably think they are fairly easy to remember—unless you're scared out of your mind as I was the first time I went climbing.

Sometimes when I'm really nervous and can't remember what I'm supposed to say, I make things up. That's what happened that first day. I was belaying, and although I wasn't the one climbing, it would be my turn to climb next, and that was unnerving. My partner was ready, and said "On belay." I responded appropriately with "Belay on."

So far, so good. But when my partner said, "Climbing!" and I realized that I was going to be responsible for this person's life, I totally locked up. It created an embarrassing silence. When he turned to look at me, I just blurted out, "Climb strong!" It came out more like a question, but I thought it was pretty close to what I was supposed to say and it sort of rhymed. When my partner gave me an odd look, I knew that he knew I was petrified. All he said was, "That's a new one." I'm sure he saw my confidence start to crumble, so he quickly added, "I like it; it's different. But please say it like you mean it."

I took that as a serious vote of confidence, so I said in my bravest voice, "Climb strong!" Both of us still use that when we climb, and we now hear others saying it too. I like it because it sums it all up: the excitement, the fear, the determination, the confidence, the trust, and the thrill of going for it. "Climb strong!" is how I end every program, and it's on all my marketing materials. I've taught my boys to use it when they climb. It's special to me and another of my courage touchstones, and it will always remind me to act with courage and conviction.

Your Response to Critical Question #14: How Will I Climb Strong?

This critical question started out as, "Will you climb strong?" Then I realized that the question phrased that way had a yes or no answer. That wasn't good enough because everyone would probably answer yes. The real question is how you will ensure that you start and continue to climb strong!

Making a conscious decision to climb strong and then thinking through your strategy for how you will accomplish this is one more critical piece of the process. It is one way smart women use their passion to seize the day.

Critical Question #15
What Am I Waiting For?

Not believing in yourself may be the greatest risk you'll ever take.

The National Anthem

Janece, who worked in the state government, was attending one of my programs. Her mountain was to start a wedding planning business, but she felt she didn't have the courage to start. When I asked her why she had chosen that particular business, she said she just loved everything about weddings; in fact, she often sang at weddings. Some of Janece's coworkers were nearby, and they all started talking about how talented she was. Out of the blue, I asked her if she'd sing something for us.

Janece came up to the front of the room, got on stage, took the microphone, and with no advanced warning, no preparation, and no accompaniment sang "The Star-Spangled Banner." It was the most beautiful and the most moving rendition of our national anthem that I have ever heard. Nearly everyone in the room (all women) had tears in their eyes when she finished. It was truly an amazing experience.

Clearly risk is subjective. There is no way I would have been willing to stand up in front of a group and sing anything. I do not have the courage, talent, or passion. My guess is that out of a couple of hundred people, no one else in that room would have been willing to take the risk of singing either. Yet many of us in that room would and have taken the risk of starting our own business—the risk that Julie was afraid to take. Risk taking is a fascinating subject.

The most amazing thing of all was that at the end of the program, three women came up to Julie and asked her to call them because each was planning a wedding: they wanted to help her start her business—another example of how taking a risk based on your passion creates new opportunities.

By declaring your mountain and taking a risk, doors open. Interestingly it's hard to tell who is going to help you as you climb your mountain. Sometimes it's family, sometimes it's friends, and sometimes all those people you thought you could count on fade away. But just then, along comes a stranger, an angel, someone to help you. The key is that no one can help you climb if you're not out there on your mountain trying.

What to Do When You Don't Know What to Do

What should you do when you don't know what to do? If you truly don't know what move to make, try to give yourself some time to think it through. If you don't have that luxury, then the best course of action is to trust your instinct. There is no one else who knows the situation better than you, so act on your intuition. You will most likely do the right thing for the right reason and in the smartest way. Then you can always trust that you've done the best you could at the time with what you knew.

Your Response to Critical Question #15: What Am I Waiting For?

Now it's time for you to decide if you're ready, if you're excited to begin. If not, look closely at what is still holding you back, and find a way to use your passion to push through your fears. If you are ready, put down this book and start climbing.

■ ■ ■

Your Mountain Is Waiting

Risk is not an opportunity to be avoided.
Risk is an unavoidable opportunity.

As you attempt new things, you find new talents. As you find new talents, you discover greater success. With greater success, your confidence builds. As you become more confident, you're willing to risk new things. This, in essence, is the positive risk cycle. The reality is that if you choose the right risk and take it in the smartest way possible, even if that risk doesn't turn out as planned, it will still turn out by creating a new opportunity.

> If you underestimate yourself,
> then you are overestimating the risk.

Positive risk allows you to see the possibilities in yourself as well as the world around you. It allows you to tap into your core strengths, talents, and passions so that you can push through your fears and climb with conviction. The best risk you can ever take is to believe in yourself. I believe in you. Your mountain is waiting.

Climb strong!

Epilogue:
The Next Horizon

What do you see when you
get to the top of a mountain?

More mountains.

Once you've finished your climb, it is time to rest, renew, and reflect. At the end of any adventure, no matter the outcome, you have changed, and it's time to ask yourself in the light of positive risk:

- ✓ What did I learn?
- ✓ What wisdom did I gain?
- ✓ What did I do well?
- ✓ What would I do again?
- ✓ What would I change?
- ✓ What memories will I cherish?
- ✓ What stories will make me laugh?

It's now time to recalibrate. That requires understanding how you've changed and incorporating those changes into your life in a positive way. Then it will be time to think about the next horizon. What's out there next for you? What has your passion now? All of us at different points in our lives struggle with the question, "What's next?" Astronauts and Olympic athletes often face depression because they aren't sure what they should do once they've walked on the moon or won a gold medal.

The key to risk taking is that the more risks you take, the more you learn. The more you learn, the better you become at taking risks. The better you get, the more confidence you gain. The more confidence you gain, the more courage you have. The more courage you have, the better you get at taking risks.

This book isn't about taking risks just for the sake of taking risks. It's about awakening the leader within so that you see your potential as well as your ability to climb those mountains that will make a difference in your life.

Appendix A: Positive Risk Checklist

A life spent in making mistakes is not
only more honorable but more useful
than a life spent in doing nothing.
—*George Bernard Shaw*

IntelligentRisking simplifies the often complicated and convoluted process of risk taking. This
book blends the "want to" of positive risk with
the "how to" of IntelligentRisking.

We've explored the four IntelligentRisking
strategies and the fifteen critical questions. In
life, there are no right or wrong answers. There is
no foolproof system to know for sure if you are
taking the right risk. However, the thought process
explored in this book regarding your mountain,

your route, your courage, and how you'll climb dramatically increases your odds for success.

In an effort to simplify the process further, this appendix summarizes the fifteen critical questions to ask before you risk. Use this as a checklist to ensure that you've considered your risk from a variety of perspectives. If there are any that you're unsure of, use the cross-reference so that you can quickly review that section.

This review is a quick, concise tool that you can use to help you climb all the mountains you face in your life.

Strategy I: Choose Your Mountain

Critical Question #1:
What's My Mountain?

After you have looked at and reviewed all of the possibilities, decide on the goal, challenge, or dream that you want to pursue. (Refer to page 87 for more information.)

Critical Question #2:
Whose Mountain Is It?

Now that you have chosen your goal, you must ask yourself if you are honestly climbing this mountain for yourself or to please someone else. (Refer to page 109 for more information.)

Critical Question #3: How Do I Define Success?

Clarify how you define success as it relates to all aspects of your life: professional, personal, financial, emotional, physical, and spiritual. (Refer to page 116 for more information.)

Strategy II: Plan Your Route

Critical Question #4: What's My Route?

Create a route that capitalizes on your positive core with built-in flexibility. Take the time to think through your plan based on the Intelligent-Risking foundation of who, what, when, where, how, and why. The more significant the risk is, the more detailed your plan should be. (Refer to page 127 for more information.)

Critical Question #5: What's My Contingency Plan?

Design a backup for the critical components of your plan. Build contingencies for anything that might stop you if things don't go according to your original plan. (Refer to page 144 for more information.)

Strategy III: Build Your Courage

Critical Question #6: How Do I Visualize Success?

Create a compelling future for yourself by developing a vivid, compelling, and powerful visualization so powerful that you'll be irresistibly drawn toward it. (Refer to page 155 for more information.)

Critical Question #7: What Are My Passions?

Determine what genuine passions you have around this reward. Think through what it is that you care about and why it matters so much to you. Constantly look for ways to increase your passion. (Refer to page 160 for more information.)

Critical Question #8: What Are My Fears?

List the fears you have that lay behind this risk by asking, "What truly is the worst that could happen?" Find ways to reduce your fears. (Refer to page 170 for more information.)

Critical Question #9: What Are My Invisible Risks and Rewards?

Uncover what hidden risks and rewards are involved with this mountain. Ask, "What if I do?" and "What if I don't?" to help you identify your risk and rewards. (Refer to page 175 for more information.)

Critical Question #10: What's My Courage Ratio?

Determine if your passion is great enough to push through your fears. If it is, then you'll have the courage to act. (Refer to page 178 for more information.)

Critical Question #11: What's My Courage Touchstone?

Choose a person, place, poem, or memory to help you reconnect with your courage when you find yourself listening to the monster within. (Refer to page 181 for more information.)

Strategy IV: Climb Strong!

Critical Question #12: What Do I Need to Let Go?

In climbing, you must let go to make your next move. Determine what it is that you need to let go so that you can move forward. (Refer to page 189 for more information.)

Critical Question #13: How Will I Embrace My Adventure?

It is always your choice as to how you'll climb your mountain. You'll build strength with a positive, flexible, and resourceful attitude. It's up to you to keep a bright heart and make your climb fun. (Refer to page 192 for more information.)

Critical Question #14: How Will I Climb Strong?

"Climb strong!" sums it all up: the excitement, the fear, the determination, the confidence, the trust, and the thrill of going for it. Every climb starts with one step, which creates the momentum for the rest of your climb. Use your passion to seize the day. (Refer to page 195 for more information.)

Critical Question #15: What Am I Waiting For?

Now it's time for you to decide if you're ready, if you're excited to begin. If not, look closely at what is still holding you back and find a way to use your passion to push through your fears. (Refer to page 200 for more information.)

Appendix B:
Best Practices

Somewhere out in this audience
may even be someone who will one
day follow my footsteps and preside over
the White House as the president's
spouse. I wish him well!

—*Barbara Bush*

The material presented in this appendix supports yet is not a critical part of the IntelligentRisking for women process. It explores the what, why, and how behind men and women's leadership styles regarding risk taking.

Best practices is a composite of successful leadership styles for both men and women, with the intent of learning which, if any, we may want to incorporate into our own leadership style. We also look at some of the basic differences between how men and women view risk, why these differences exist, and how to deal with them.

There is enormous value in understanding and developing your own individual leadership style—one that feels natural and complements your own personality. This is true whether you have a thousand people reporting to you or if the only person reporting to you is you.

I met Cynthia Comparin, chief executive officer and president of her own company, Animato, at a networking weekend the Jackson Walker law firm sponsored in San Antonio. Animato is a $100 million business that focuses on people and technology in motion. It specializes in financial and human resource management software.

Cynthia is a dynamo focused on the big picture. Over dinner, her friends teased her about how she doesn't like to be bothered with the details to the point that Sheila, her personal assistant, virtually runs her life for her. I asked Cynthia how she came to start a business that is all about details when she so obviously disliked doing detail work. Her answer was that as a former group chief financial officer for EDS, she learned how to do detail better than anyone.

Cynthia explained that although that detail mind-set is not her natural style, she saw it as the price of admission to play the game. It was the foundation she needed to launch her own new game. She still likes, wants, needs, and expects detail from those who work for her, but now she can move beyond doing details herself to focus on her strength: strategic business development.

The irony is that before you can move into your own natural style, you must earn the right by being good at what you do, and to get good at what you do, you must understand what leadership skills are required to build your own foundation. Some of those may come naturally, and some may not. This is when you must decide to accept, reject, or change to include those other traits. As with almost everything else in life, developing your own leadership style is a dynamic process that evolves.

When deciding if you want to adapt the leadership traits required for success within your organization, one question to ask is whether they are positive, healthy traits. Most of the time they will be; however, it's important to stay true to yourself. That is exactly how Cynthia Cooper of WorldCom, Coleen Rowley of the FBI, and Sherron Watkins of Enron landed on the cover of *Time* magazine as Persons of the Year in 2002. They were not willing to accept or adapt to what their organizations demanded and instead held true to themselves and became whistle-blowers.

I recently had a conversation about this subject with a friend of mine, Debra Baldwin, a senior vice president at the University of Phoenix, the largest private university in the world. She has a wealth of professional experience and has been a key player in helping the University of Phoenix achieve its phenomenal growth. In 2002 she was selected as a Woman of Distinction by the Mile High Council of Girl Scouts. In 2003, she was chosen as one of the Outstanding Women in Business by the *Denver Business Journal.*

When Debra and I began discussing this subject, I asked her what advice she gives other women regarding leadership and risk. Her response was immediate: "Live a balanced life that allows you to celebrate your full potential in every aspect of what is vital to you; that *will* require some degree of risk. Success often means the risk of criticism. It is hard to be invisible and lead at the same time. Exposure to criticism is the cost of admission to top levels of the organization, so risk intelligently. Never compromise ethics, integrity, values, matters of compliance, or the hearts and minds of others. Most important, never ever settle for a mediocre life."

Gender Difference Theories

The most successful managers in the future will be those who are willing to go beyond their own comfort zones and take the risk of expanding their professional competencies to include skills from both male and female perspectives. They are the ones who will bring value to their organizations and develop the intellectual capital and management talent that they can capitalize on in any environment. Since there are not too many men's groups requesting programs on this topic, we'll focus on how we as women can become more successful leaders.

Many theories have been offered as to why there are gender differences in leadership. The two most prevalent are the psychological and situational theories. The psychological theory emphasizes the different outlook, attitudes, and values implanted in men and women during their development and socialization. Women tend to demonstrate greater affiliation, attachment, cooperation, and nurturance, while men tend to demonstrate more independent, instrumentally oriented, and competitive behaviors.

The situational theory argues that gender differences are few and largely an artifact of differences in opportunity, power, and lack of representation in business and organizational settings. I'm convinced that the reality lies in a combination of the two.

Still other theories propose that there are no differences between men and women and that it all comes down to the differences between individuals. However, being a mother of three teenage boys, I can tell you that based on firsthand experience, there are many, many distinctive differences between males and females. Testosterone literally drips off the walls at my house. A typical conversation with my boys goes something like this:

Mom: Why did you push him?
Son: He was standing there.

Mom: Can't we just enjoy the game?
Son: It's not fun if you don't win.

Mom: We need to talk about this.
Son: There's nothing to talk about.

A tremendous amount of research has been done by qualified individuals on the differences between men and women and why more capable women are not achieving higher levels of success in businesses. I've done a significant amount of quantitative and qualitative research, in addition to reading dozens of books and hundreds of articles on the subject. Yet whenever I hear someone touting research statistics, I'm reminded of the old adage, "Figures don't lie, liars figure." I don't mean to imply that everyone is intentionally skewing the results to support their own theory. We just seem to have a way of making information fit our needs. Even when results are reported accurately, you still can't always trust what people say they will do in a given situation.

In one situation I encountered at Mattel Toys, I was involved in new product development, and since traditional toys were appealing to a younger and younger audience, we were losing a significant amount of market share.

We were trying to develop products that would appeal to older children. One was to develop a funky boom box. Market research at the time was huge at Mattel, so we brought in a number of teenagers and asked them their opinions of what features they felt kids would want in a product.

One specific question we asked was, "What color would sell the most?" Their overwhelming response was neon "hot" green. At the end of the session, as they were leaving, we invited them to take a boom box as a thank-you gift for their time. Every one of them took a black one. From that day on, I've always said, "There is research, and then there is research. There is what we say we'll do in any given situation, and then there is what we actually do." Each of us needs to come up with our own conclusions regarding the information others propose based on what rings true to us.

Based on what I have experienced, what others have experienced, and what I've studied, I don't believe that any one theory explains gender differences. I think that a multitude of factors combine in unique ways that contribute to our struggle to find meaningful success. They come into play in different combinations according to the situation at the time. They also vary in degree based on our specific industry, company, team, environment, background, experience, and personality. Some of these factors are within our control, and some are not.

For the purposes of this book, I've chosen to concentrate on two reasons behind some of the more significant gender differences: (1) the continued gulf in the understanding of the differences between men and women in business and (2) the need for women to take intelligent risks. I've chosen these two because they are both extremely important, highly pervasive, and within our control.

Women are a talented, creative pool of talent. We represent an incredible amount of intellectual capital. Corporations and other companies are beginning to understand that they have made a tremendous investment in us and can no longer afford to lose us to other companies or careers by not meeting our needs. They understand that it is through accumulating and holding on to this intellectual capital that they'll be able to establish and maintain their competitive edge. They're now becoming focused on finding a way to make it work. For forward-thinking organizations such as Deloitte & Touche and Equity Office Properties, it has become a business imperative because they are now correlating diversity success with increased profits to the bottom line.

Because organizations are beginning to understand what a valuable resource we are, it's now up to us to understand what we want and achieve the kinds of meaningful success we're after.

Successful Leadership Traits:
Men

Men do a lot of things right, so let's take a look at what leadership traits we most admire and respect from our male counterparts. As we look at some of the differences between men and women, I will be making some broad generalizations. Some of what I discuss will be true about some men all the time, all men some of the time, and no man all of the time. There is no intent to show any lack of respect or admiration for our male counterparts. I hope you (as well as the many males reading this) will accept these generalizations of both men and women in the spirit in which they are intended.

Given all the disclaimers, groups usually come up with a similar list of qualities that we admire about men as listed below. You may want to add some of your own thoughts about the qualities and characteristics that you admire. In general men can be:

✓ Detached (they don't take things too personally; they can disagree and fight during a meeting and still go out for a beer together)

✓ Big-picture oriented

✓ Competitive and assertive

✓ Risk takers

✓ Individualistic

✓ Work hard and play hard

✓ Networkers (old boys' clubs)

✓ Self-promoters (talking about their accomplishments)

✓ Objective and not overly emotional

✓ Success oriented (clear on their goal)

✓ Direct (they ask for what they want and expect to get it)

✓ Focused

Women

Women share many of the traits listed for men; however, there are some traits that are unique to us. Let's look at what we admire and respect the most about ourselves. If I've missed anything, include it on your own list. In general women can be:

✓ Sensitive

✓ Intuitive

✓ Empathetic

✓ Flexible

✓ Team players, collaborative

✓ Hard workers

✓ Nurturing

✓ Modest

✓ Passionate

✓ Effective communicators

✓ Good listeners and tactful

✓ Multitaskers

Let me mention here that women have come a long way. A study published by the *Harvard Business Review* in 1965 entitled "Are Women Executives People?" showed that 32 percent of all male managers believed that women's fundamental biological makeup made them unfit for management.[1]

My first professional job was with Hallmark Cards, and I was in the Chicago branch office. I was at that time the only woman in any type of management position. All the other women in the office were secretaries. It was 1974, and if there was a meeting, I automatically got everyone coffee. I did this of my own free will. No one asked me to; in fact, it would never have crossed the men's minds to ask me, but it was just expected. I wasn't resentful because I didn't know any better. Two years later, I felt differently. I made the decision that I would no longer get everyone's coffee. I felt that by taking a stand, I was taking a risk. Today this would never be an issue.

My friend Valari recalls that she was delighted when she was offered a position with Mattel Toys in 1968. It was a sales position and considered a plum job with a great company. It was during a time when most women with careers were secretaries, nurses, teachers, or stewardesses. Those were the norms. Period.

Valari was given the title of "retail specialist," a sales territory, and a sales goal. After a short training period and a few sales meetings later, she realized that all the other women working in sales were "retail specialists" while the men with the same job were called "retail merchandisers." Although the job, the territories, the sales goals, and the expectations were the same for both, the retail specialists were "nonexempt" while the retail merchandisers were "exempt." This meant that although they were doing the same job, the men were given company cars, higher wages, and more benefits.

This struck Valari and most of the other women as unjust and discriminatory. However, because most of the women were grateful to have this job, no one wanted to create a wave and rock the boat. That was until a sales meeting when the senior vice president of sales and marketing asked Valari how she enjoyed her job. Before answering, she realized she had a choice. She could say the politically right thing or take a risk and tell the truth: that she felt it was unfair that women were doing the same job as the men for substantially lower pay and benefits.

She took the risk and outlined exactly how she felt, at the same time wondering where she'd be working next. She didn't lose her job. In fact, at the next sales meeting, the same senior vice president made the announcement that all sixty of the retail specialists were being promoted to retail merchandisers.

Unfortunately, it remains tough in the business world for women. It's hard to get equal opportunities and equal pay, particularly at the higher levels. Like it or not, the game is still dominated and run by men with a man's mind-set, predispositions, and prejudices. That is why often men are judged on their potential and women judged on their performance. It's helpful to understand why and how to operate in this environment.

The Differences

The preceding lists of qualities contain some opposing qualities that are on both lists as traits we respect. For example, we admire men's ability to self-promote, yet we respect our ability to be modest. We like the assertive nature of men, but we're proud of our ability to nurture.

The differences in what we admire can be confusing. Some of us have been coached along the way to "blow our own horn" more often. Sometimes it works, and sometimes it blows up in our face. Why? Significant research has been done that makes a substantial case for how being more assertive works for women. Then again, it has been equally substantiated by research that being assertive doesn't work for women. With so much conflicting information, what are we to do? The key is to be assertive in a way that feels natural and plays into your own individual style. Don't force it. If it doesn't work for you, then it won't feel right to anyone else.

It may help to take a look at some of the reasons we're so different from men. Recently I took my oldest son, Connor, on a business trip with me to Boston, and one evening we went to see Rob Becker's show, *Defending the Caveman,* an extremely funny take on the differences between men and women.

In the show, he asks the audience to imagine six men sitting around a bowl of chips. One of them says to the others, "Hey, we're out of chips." How many men jump up to fill the bowl? Of course, you already know: none. We have now stepped into the world of male negotiation, which goes something like this. Male 1 says, "I'm not going to get the chips; I filled the bowl the first time." Male 2 responds, "Well, I'm not going to get them; I brought the bowl." Male 3 counters with, "I'm not going to get them; I brought the beer." Says Male 4, "I'm not going to get them; it's my house." On it goes until one of three things happens: they all starve to death, one poor soul finally gives in, or the host's wife comes in and makes him do it. Either way, the man who has to get more chips is the loser. Even so, there are no hard feelings, no grudges, between the men.

Now imagine six women sitting around the chip bowl. Someone mentions they're out of chips. How many women get up to fill the bowl? Of course, all six. And if one didn't? What if one woman sat there and waited while all the others got up? She'd be the loser, though a loser of a different kind. We all know the rules for this type of social interaction. In the end, whether it's a group of men or a group of women, the chip bowl usually gets refilled, but it's a perfect example of the differences between men and women.

As my son and I watched the rest of the show, we both laughed until we had tears running down our faces. (Editorial correction requested by my son: I had tears running down my face, and he just had something in his eye.)

Teams versus Individuals

Today's organizations talk about teams, but most still reward individuals. Women tend to talk in terms of "we," while men talk in terms of "I." We make a tactical decision for the good of the project, and we share information and resources, but instead of being looked on as a strategic team player, we're called "nice." Women are good at relationship skills, but this is often misunderstood and viewed as "women being friendly." If a woman makes a decision based on her instinct, she does not get the same respect as a man making a decision based on his instinct.

Young boys get together and immediately start bragging about who's the best, who should be the leader. They start reliving their exploits and retelling their successes. They tell each other that they're the smartest, the strongest, and on and on. Finally someone is chosen to be the leader. They start the game King of the Hill, and the rest of the boys try to push the leader off of the hill so that they can be king.

Imagine a group of young girls getting together and one of them saying, "I think I should be the leader because I'm the smartest [or the strongest or the most beautiful or something else]." She'd be seen as pushy and arrogant. How long would she even be allowed in the group?

Through games like King of the Hill, boys learn to promote their strengths and at all costs hide their weaknesses. A show of weakness means an attack from the group. Women, in contrast, learn how to be inclusive by playing down their strengths and being open about their weaknesses.[2]

My boys were fighting the other day. When I came into the room to find out what was going on, one of them said, "He started it when he hit me back." I realized that this is the universal way boys and men look at the world (and I personally believe it accounts for how they get into so many wars).

Self-Promotion versus Modesty

When I started speaking about IntelligentRisking, I said very little about my professional experiences with Coors, Disney, Hallmark, and Mattel. I was afraid that I'd appear too egocentric if I talked about myself. My clients were confused and disappointed. They had to point out to me that the reason they hired me was so that I would share some of my successes. It's amazing how ingrained humility is in women. Although it's something we admire, it can get in our way.

Psychologist Laurie Heatherington and her colleagues asked hundreds of incoming college students to predict what grades they would get in their first year. Some subjects were asked to make their predictions privately by writing them down and placing them in an envelope; others were asked to make their predictions publicly, in the presence of a researcher. The results showed that more women than men predicted lower grades for themselves if they made their predictions publicly. If they made their predictions privately, the predictions were the same as those of the men and the same as their actual grades. What could have been interpreted as a lack of confidence was actually the act of being modest.[3]

Minimizing Doubts versus Maximizing Certainty

My brother, Doug, has always said, "Better to be thought a fool than to open your mouth and prove it." This provides a powerful insight into why men don't ask for directions: if they ask, they prove they don't know something and thus reveal a weakness.

It's important for women to understand how men view others who ask questions. If you are in a meeting and ask lots of questions, men generally will assume you don't know as much as those who aren't asking questions. This may or may not be true. It may be that the others are just too afraid to ask. I have also found that women tend to ask questions for clarification, not because they don't know, and to help out others if they feel not everyone understands.

Women are quick to say, "I'm sorry," while a man is quick to say, "I'll accept your apology." It's very difficult for a man to admit fault if he doesn't have to. This all comes back to men's conditioning to play up their strengths and hide any and all of their weaknesses. A man equates revealing a weakness as leaving himself vulnerable to an attack.

Competitive Ritual versus Complimentary Ritual

Many men have their rituals of combat. They love to spar in a meeting. They like to throw out an idea (it might even be one they don't really even believe in), heatedly argue it, and then go out together for a beer. Most women don't get this. We want to be able to do that and not take any of it personally, but it isn't what we're used to.

We do, however, have our rituals of compliments. Let's imagine that Linda walks up to JoAnn and says, "Your hair looks great today." JoAnn responds to Linda and says, "I love that new jacket. You look great in it." All women know how this ritual works. Men seldom understand this ritual.

In the business world, this ritual of compliments works a little differently because it collides with a man's tendency to look for a one-up position. A friend of mine was part of a team that flew to New York to give a major client presentation. She thought everyone had done a good job with their presentation but felt that hers was the best. Her boss had even told her that she had done the best job.

On the return flight to Los Angeles, she sat next to a male associate. Once they were settled on the plane, she turned to him and said something like, "I thought you did a really good job on your presentation." He said, "Thank you." Then she waited. We all know what he was supposed to say, right? But he didn't. He said nothing. That was when my friend made a huge tactical error by asking, "What did you think of my presentation?" He then launched into a two-hour evaluation of her presentation and what she should have done differently. He took the one-up position that she had handed him. Next time she'll be much clearer about what she wants by asking, "What did you like about my presentation?"

This story is a good example of how men are conditioned to quickly accept compliments, whether they deserve them or not. I'm convinced this is a huge asset. Women, in comparison, have been conditioned to play down, deny, or even reject compliments, even when they are well deserved. I was told the story of a professional singer, a woman with a strikingly beautiful voice who says that the hardest thing for her after a performance is to thank those who compliment her because her instinct is always to start talking about what was wrong with her performance. This reaction goes back to our early years, when we wanted to fit in and find ways to be inclusive. By the time we're adults, we all know better. As I talk to senior professional women all over the country, they assure me that they are way beyond this challenge. They all tell me that they are just as quick as a man to accept a compliment. Well, maybe they are, and maybe they aren't.

I was having breakfast with my friend Leslie Carlson, who at the time was the vice president of operations for Destination Hotels & Resorts in Denver. We were talking about this very subject when another friend of mine approached our table with her husband to say hello. As I was introducing Leslie, I mentioned that she was a marketing genius. Leslie's immediate response was, "No, I'm not." The immediate reaction of my friend's husband was to say, "I have never received a compliment like that in my life; you should accept it." I'm convinced that these social patterns run more deeply than we believe.

Focus on Success versus Focus on Failure

Check a man's to-do list, and it may have 10 things on it. Check a woman's to-do list, and it may have 110 things on it. At the end of the day if a man gets 7 things done, he is proud of himself. He may take the evening off and celebrate in some way. At the end of the day if we look at our list and we've accomplished 95 things, how often do we take the evening off to bask in our success? Never. We don't take a single minute to tell anyone about all that we've accomplished. Instead we work until we drop into bed exhausted but dwelling on those 5 things we didn't get done. This is not healthy. The ability to focus on success is embedded in men from an early age. This is a skill women need to acquire.

Not only do we focus on what we didn't get done, we have a tendency to devalue our own accomplishments. So in addition to focusing on what we didn't get done, we tend to think that we didn't get anything important done. The reality is that we still got 95 things done; yet not only are we not giving ourselves credit for them, somehow we lose credit because those things weren't really important in our own eyes.

My research tells me that one of the key reasons we do this is that we aren't really clear on how we define success. One minute we define success in a more holistic and qualitative way, which may include a nurturing role in which we are trying to create a wholesome and delicious family meal that everyone will eat, bake cookies, run errands, chauffeur the kids, clean, and more. Then the next minute we may define success in a more quantifiable way, where we need to make a very clear, calculable difference in which we measure success by income, power, and status.

Either definition of success or a combination works very well. What doesn't work as well is when we aren't sure of how we define success or we rely on someone else's definition of success for us. What happens then is that we swing back and forth between definitions. If this happens, we find ourselves getting 95 things done during the day that are important to us, and yet at the end of the day, when we start looking for quantifiable, measurable successes, we come up short. It is critical that we are clear on how we define success.

One week after attending my IntelligentRisking program, a woman e-mailed me saying that it had taken her ten years to get the vice presidency that she wanted and one week to figure out that wasn't what she really wanted at all. The fact that women own 66 percent of all home-based business reinforces that we struggle to find success in a traditional environment and have decided to find success on our own terms.

This tendency of ours to downplay our successes is the reason I want you to list every one of your strengths and only a few of your weaknesses. If I don't ask women to look at their leadership style in this way, they often end up focusing on the negatives. Yet to be successful at anything, it helps to visualize yourself as successful.

Setting Yourself Up for Success versus Setting Yourself Up Not to Fail

Situational theories certainly come into play. It is naturally easier for men to understand men than it is for men to understand women. This holds true in reverse. Given that the majority of senior positions are held by men, it is easier for them to imagine how a man with a wife and three children can get the job done than it is for them to imagine how a woman with a husband and three children can get the job done. Let's face it: most women still bear the responsibility of keeping up the home and raising the children. So with all the qualifications being equal, the edge will usually go to the man.

Many men hesitate to give a woman a plum assignment, believing that women end up leaving the company to have children. The woman, fully qualified for these assignments, sees herself passed up time and time again, gets frustrated, and leaves the company. Her manager then says, "I told you so."

At the same time, women often set up their own scenarios for failure. I regularly hear women saying that they were offered a promotion and weren't sure they were ready for it. Because they didn't want to set themselves up for failure, they passed up the opportunity, only to watch a man with less knowledge, talent, and experience come in and take the job.

IntelligentRisking

One key to IntelligentRisking is self-confidence, because no one can predict the course or outcome of a risk. That means that to risk, you must have a significant amount of confidence and be willing to trust your own ability and resourcefulness to see the risk through, no matter what.

I'm often asked if men have a better knack for taking risks. My answer is, "No, they do not." However, they are often more willing to take risks because of their high self-confidence. They have spent their lives focusing on their strengths and enhancing them. They have spent a lifetime minimizing their weaknesses. They have been conditioned to be competitive and fight for their ideas. They constantly visualize themselves as King of the Hill.

The reality is that people (men or women) who continually see themselves in this type of successful light tend to have more confidence, real or imagined, so they are more willing to give it a go. The goal of this book is to help women see that they already have what it takes. The key is for us to focus on our strengths, be clear about what we want, and practice IntelligentRisking.

Women want to contribute in an effective and meaningful way without losing ourselves. We know we're bright enough. We know we have the education. We know we have the tools we need. The irony is that we women have what we need to risk, and yet it is difficult to hold on to the self-confidence we require if we underplay our successes, devalue our accomplishments, and sell ourselves short. These tendencies create a phenomenon where women who have the talent, the skill, and the courage to risk hold back because they can't see their own potential.

Positive Risk for Women

Positive risk is intended to help you set yourself up for success. The reality is that we have what it takes to be successful. All we need is to see the possibilities within ourselves and focus on our core strengths, talents, and passions while we take intelligent risks. I wish you the best of luck with all the mountains in your life. Climb strong!

Notes

Chapter Two

1. S. Brzowsky, "How to Be Stress-Resilient," *Parade Magazine,* Oct. 12, 2003, pp. 10–12.

2. D. Jones, "Few Women Hold Top Executive Jobs, Even When CEO's Are Female," *USA Today,* Jan. 27, 2003, p. 1B.

3. M. Heffernan, "The Female CEO ca. 2002," *Fast Company,* no. 61, Aug. 2002, p. 58. http://www.fastcompany.com/online/61/female_ceo.html.

4 S. A. Hewlett, "Executive Women and the Myth of Having It All," *Harvard Business Review,* Apr. 2002, pp. 5–11.

5. Hewlett, "Executive Women and the Myth of Having It All."

6. Heffernan, "The Female CEO."

Chapter Seven

1. B. Breen, "Desire: Connecting with What Customers Want," *Fast Company,* Feb. 2003, p. 86.

Chapter Nine

1. The breakthrough in Dr. Leuchter's study was not that placebos worked for some patients. The breakthrough came in what he discovered about how the

brain works. Patients taking both real medication and placebos came in for regular EEGs to see if the researchers could detect any early changes in the brain waves. They were looking to identify a brain wave signature that would predict if an antidepressant would help. They ended up finding some interesting and opposing patterns in the patients who improved whether they were on antidepressants or placebos. Dr. Leuchter's study gave quantifiable evidence to what we intuitively believe: there is amazing power in just the thought or expectation that you are going to feel better. Our brains are amazingly complex, and clearly there are multiple pathways to healing.

Chapter Ten

1. L. Day, *The Circle* (New York: Penguin Putnam, 2001).

Appendix B

1. G. W. Bowman, N. B. Worthy, and S. A. Greyser, "Are Women Executives People?" *Harvard Business Review,* 1965, *43,* 15–28, 164–178.

2. For more on this, read D. Tannen, *The Power of Talk: Who Gets Heard and Why* (Boston: Harvard Business School Press, 2002).

3. Cited in Tannen, *The Power of Talk.*

Acknowledgments

A special acknowledgment to Valari Burger: Valari has read and reread this book almost as many times as I have. She is, without a doubt, the only reason this book ever made it to print. It is through her that I understand what true friendship, loyalty, and commitment mean. Her faith and confidence in me continue to be unwavering. Today more than ever before, she is my twin spirit. Thank you, Valari, for being my courage touchstone and staying close to me even now.

A special acknowledgment to my sons, Nick, Joey, and Connor: I admire each of you for your individual strength of character and unique approach to life. The three of you have kept me humble, shown me how to play, and taught me about unconditional love. You have provided me with limitless stories as well as given me tremendous insights into the power of staying positive and the differences between men and women. Those fabulous hugs of yours give me courage; thank you.

A special acknowledgment to Brian O'Malley: Brian is a former police officer, SWAT team member, and paramedic firefighter, as well as a Mount Everest climber, award-winning photographer, author, and world-renowned lecturer. That's quite a background to bring to a conversation regarding risk. Many of the concepts in this book were born out of the lively, heated debates we have had over the years regarding how men and women look at risk differently. I must admit it's hard to argue too fiercely with the guy who's holding the rope while you climb. Brian, I thank you for being my climbing partner and providing me with a solid foundation with your patience, support, and inspiration.

October 2005   Barbara Stoker
Centennial, Colorado

The Author

BARBARA STOKER, author of *A Woman with a Minute . . .* (2006) and *IntelligentRisking for Women* (2004), has been an executive for Disney, Hallmark, Mattel, and Coors. Now she is one of the most influential thinkers on personal leadership and risk, specializing in women and risk taking. Stoker's expertise goes beyond her professional experience. Her personal adventures include being an avid technical rock and ice climber, as well as a paragliding pilot. In addition, she is the single mother of three sons, well acquainted with the difficult choices and risks women face as they manage their multidimensional lives. Stoker was selected by the *Rocky Mountain News* in 2002 as "50 & Fabulous" based on the nomination of her three sons. She is also a wish grantor for the Make-A-Wish Foundation.

For over a decade, Stoker has been speaking on the subject of risk, creativity, and team development, using an appreciative inquiry model. Her success on the lecture circuit is based on her dynamic, interactive style that encourages individuals to choose a mountain, rediscover their courage, tap into their wisdom, and take risks that will make a difference in their lives.

Stoker acquired her experience through a career that involved licensing several Walt Disney movies, launching Hallmark Card's Gift Business, starting Mattel Toys' collectible business by developing the Porcelain Barbie, and selling a "can't be sold" product for Coors with an opening order of $1 million.

Stoker's years of corporate experience with these four innovative Fortune 500 companies have provided her with a solid and diverse foundation that includes sales, marketing, customer service, licensing, merchandising, store design, new product development, engineering, strategic planning, and new business development. She understands professional risks and has the reputation for getting things done because of her innovative, unconventional, and often counterintuitive approach.

Stoker is on the board of directors of the Colorado Independent Publishers Association (CIPA). Her book *IntelligentRisking for Women* has won an EVVY award, the top award that CIPA presents. *A Woman with a Minute . . .* (a charming illustrated book that accurately captures the reality of life for women today) has been on the Colorado best-seller list for months.

Stoker can be reached at Barbara@Barbara Stoker.com or by calling IntelligentRisking, Inc., at 303-779-1999. For more information, visit www.BarbaraStoker.com.

Index